Five Seasons in the Kitchen

Zen Inspired Vegan Cooking | Avital Sebbag

TO SEE THE BEAUTY OF THE UNIVERSE
BETWEEN EARTH AND SKY.
A BUD APPEARS
AFTER THE RAIN
CONTAINS THE ESSENCE OF LIFE
SO PURE AND FRESH
SEASONS GO
SEASONS COME.

AVITAL SEBBAG

For my parents, Gabriel (of Blessed Memory)
and Simcha Sebbag who gave me life.
For my sons Yossi, Mikey, Gabriel (Babi),
Joey and Jonathan.

五穀味津

Photography
Michal Lenart

Hebrew Editor
Tamar Mor-Sela

English Translation
Elizabeth Zauderer

Art and Design
Eddie Goldfine

Consultants
Efrat Marciano
Orit Rachmani

Styling
Ingrid Kutner

Calligraphy
Elsa Foyn

Layout
Itzik Yefet
Daniel Weizner

Five Seasons in the Kitchen
Zen Inspired Vegan Cooking

AVITAL SEBBAG

Five Seasons in the Kitchen
Zen Inspired Vegan Cooking
AVITAL SEBBAG

Published by: Avitality, Domain of Change
Translated from Hebrew by: Elizabeth Zauderer

ISBN 978-965-550-580-1

Copyright © 2015 by Avital Sebbag, Tel Aviv

All rights reserved. This book or any portion thereof may not be reproduced or used in any manner whatsoever without the express written permission of the publisher except for the use of brief quotations in a book review.

Printed in Israel by: Ravgon Printing House, Ltd.

TABLE OF CONTENTS

|10-11| Introduction
|12-15| What is Zen?
|16-17| Seasons of the Year
|18-53| Spring
|54-89| Summer
|90-123| Late Summer
|124-151| Autumn
|152-189| Winter
|190-191| Mindful Eating
|192-205| Index
|206-207| Thanks

Introduction

This book marks a mile stone on my journey toward an understanding of heathy nutrition and its place in our lives. It is an opportunity for you, dear readers, to glimpse the wonders of a wholesome lifestyle, and to develop an awareness to the mental and spiritual benefits of well-balanced nutrition by experimenting with delicious, easy-to-prepare recipes.

This book motivates change. And change means taking action. Faced with a vast amount of information and approaches to healthy eating, you are probably wondering "What is the right way?" The truth is, there is no "right" way.

I believe with all my heart that we are all creatures of the universe whose earth, seas and skies provide us with the physical, mental and spiritual nourishment we need. That said, we must recognize the values of nature's abundant offerings, and come to know how we can best benefit from them. We must be attuned to nature, to the changing of the seasons, and with each season, to the assortment of foods it provides.

I have been practicing Zen meditation for years, and have visited many Zen monasteries around the globe. During these visits, I found myself drawn to the kitchens, the beating hearts of these establishments, where humble, tasty foods are prepared – foods that satisfy the body, while preserving the ecosystem. The practice of awareness is enhanced when foods are lighter, and so for me Zen cooking is a way to develop the essence of my existence – to contribute to the world by nurturing and nourishing myself and those around me with healthy foods, and by practicing a wholesome, happy, serene and loving lifestyle.

In 1998, I gave birth to my eldest son, the first of five boys. Motherhood radically changed my perspective on life, and deepened my desire for a well-balanced way of life in an ecologically sound environment. As a result, I embarked on an exciting exploration into the wonders of anthropological nutrition, shiatsu, Chinese medicine and Eastern philosophies. It was on these journeys that I came to understand that we are all one with the world, and that nature provides us with all we need to be healthy and happy. It is my hope that this book will encourage you to appreciate nature's gifts, to understand the importance of preserving them, and most importantly, to live your life the best way you can – after all, you too are a gift of nature.

Avital
Song Kuan

> **GOOD TO KNOW**
>
> For information on food products, recommended books and websites, mindful eating, juice cleansing and cooking techniques visit my website at www.avitality.co.il or contact me via email: avitality@gmail.com

What Is Zen?

By Sefi Rachlevski

The essence of Zen is a striving for truth beyond words; an existential and spiritual truth that any attempt to define distances one further from internalizing its core principle of liberty.

Zen was inspired by existential Taoist philosophy that developed in China approximately 2300 years ago, an age in which Buddhism was established, and in which Plato and Socrates laid the foundations of Western philosophy. This was also the time in which the Hebrew Bible canon of the Second Temple was compiled. The 'tao' in Taoism means 'path;' the leading philosopher of 'the path' was Chang Tzu.

In the following parable Chuang Tzu epitomizes the basic principle of Zen: "If the goat knew it was a goat its feet would become entangled. If the fish knew it was a fish it would sink to the bottom of the river like a lead stone. The goat, the fish, the mountain and the river know themselves by not-knowing. Only man attempts to know himself by way of a knowing. Therefore, man fails to be a man in the same way that a goat is a goat, a fish is a fish, a mountain a mountain and a river-a river."

The constant aspiration for deep knowledge, knowledge that is not founded on knowing, is the foundation of Zen philosophy. This knowledge does not scorn language and intellect, but rather searches for a path beyond definitions and social norms. An existential, internal and personal path, at the end of which is the desired 'enlightenment.' A mystical experience that hauls man out of a myriad of inner, social and definitive conflicts, and restores him to his essential existence, that which is beyond consciousness.

Zen emerged as an existential philosophy some 1500 years ago in China. From there it expanded to Japan, Korea and the rest of the world. Due to its link to Buddhism, Zen was practiced in monasteries where its objectives were to practice deep inner reflection, meditation, personal learning, a humble lifestyle and self- sustenance. Similar to the Hassidic movement at the beginning of its spiritual development, Zen focused on creativity and contemplation through short stories and dialogues. The ability of Zen to release man from his own 'internal well,' the well of words, definitions, social codes, ego, and the physical, is what attracts so many to practice it the world round.

At the opening of Marcel Proust's canonical novel "Remembrance of Things Past," the hero bites into a Madeleine cake. Its taste elicits memories and contemplations that in turn espouse memories that fill the entire novel. It is my hope that through the recipes in this book, each and every reader will find his or her own Madeleine cake. Even if it does not result in an experience of profound enlightenment, engaging with this book will at least constitute a station on a long and pleasurable existential journey of body and soul. At the end of Masehet Kidushin of the Jerusalem Talmud it says: "It is man's future to account for all that he saw and did not eat." Zen experiences itself through non-materiality and non-arrogance, but rather through the satisfying of our deepest, most genuine desires, including our desire for nutrition and nurturing. Delicious and healthy food can fill our lives with the joy of Zen.

Bon appetite!

Sefi Rachlevski

A few years ago I had the amazing opportunity of staying at Avital's home for a few days. Avital is a very vibrant and generous woman! For me, looking at a photo of one of her food creations is similar to looking at Avital, so full of crisp vitality. I was a little concerned that the menu would not contain enough protein or lack taste, but what I experienced was a significant change in how I experienced food – how it was prepared, how it tasted, and how it felt in my body.

Like many of us, I fear that raw and vegan dishes will leave me hungry or dissatisfied. By the time my visit was over, I felt nourished, energetic and grateful to Avital for introducing me to a healthier way of eating.

Zen practice teaches us to rest in the moment in order to allow our mind to open to our innate wisdom and compassion. To rest in the moment does not require any altering of our consciousness or striving for some other state of being. Zen teaches that we already contain the seeds of enlightenment and all we need to do is wake up in just this moment. This awakening allows us to see the beautiful grace and symmetry of this world.

Avital's book is a perfect example of Zen being brought forth into nutrition. Rather than altering and adding to our food, artificially coloring it or cooking the life out of it, Avital shows us how to allow food to be celebrated and honored for what it is in its natural state. We could exchange the word 'food' for the word 'mind'. We meditate to see our original mind. We eat healthy food in order to return to our original balanced and healthy self.

Soeng Hyang
Head Teacher Kwan Um School of Zen

For non-practicing people, food controls the body and the body controls the mind. For practicing people, the mind controls the body and their body controls their food. Eating healthy food just for myself is OK but it will not lead to wisdom. It can be another form of attachment to my body. Eating wisely for others becomes Great Love, Great Compassion and the Great Bodhisattva Way.

Dae Bong Sunim

Zen describes food in terms of the exquisite harmony and utter simplicity in which individual foods are arranged on the plate to express perfection. For me this was one of my first experiences of Zen – even before I began to practice Zen, I experienced it through the senses. By becoming aware of how food tapped my sense of smell, taste, touch, sound and sight, I experienced that very special "Zen ambience." In this book, Avital has meticulously collected and prepared exquisite recipes to share with us, recipes that engage all the senses and create a unique Zen ambience. Being a sincere student of Zen, I am sure Avital experienced the truth of each of her recipes and has chosen the very best for all of us to share and enjoy.

I wish all of us Zen appetite!

Jo Potter
Ji Do Poep Sa Nim

If you are looking for a book to significantly improve the quality of your life, your health, and your vitality, I highly recommend you read Five Seasons in the Kitchen and be in touch with Avital so your life can be the best life possible.

Joshua Rosenthal
MScEd, Founder/Director, Institute for Integrative Nutrition

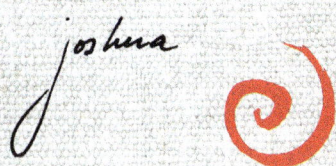

Seasons of the Year

The seasons of the year represent change. Movement. The circular progression of time is reflected in the weather, in the color of the sky, in the clouds and intensity of light, in humidity and wind factors. The seasons are stations in time. They bring with them unique sensations associated with smells, textures, colors and flavors. Living in harmony with the seasons means consuming seasonal foods that benefit body, mind and soul for an overall constellation of good health year round.

Spring

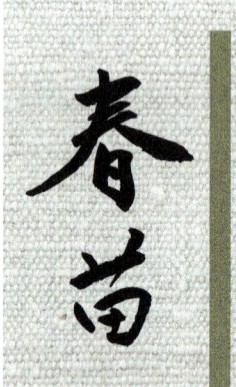

Spring is a time of light breezes, of awakening, motion and creativity. Feeding on sunlight, tiny buds quickly become beautiful blossoms – nature's expression of determination, rejuvenation, cleanliness and growth.

Organ: Liver. Detoxification and rejuvenation.

Color: Green. Stems and leaves contain chlorophyll that cleanses and strengthens body cells.

Flavor: Sour.

Foods: Lemon, vinegar, green apple, blueberry, kiwi, Swiss chard, spinach, cranberry, mallow, kumquat.

Summer

In summer nature presents itself in all its glory. It is a time of expansion and abundance. Breathtaking spectacles of blossoms and fruits express the potential stored in seeds. We are drawn outdoors to spend time with friends in an atmosphere of sharing, joy and freedom.

Organ: Heart. Communication. Circulation of oxygen-rich blood through the body.

Color: Red.

Taste: Bitter.

Foods: Cherry, watermelon, plum, peach, olives, celery and lettuce leaves, alfalfa sprouts, coffee and tea.

Late Summer

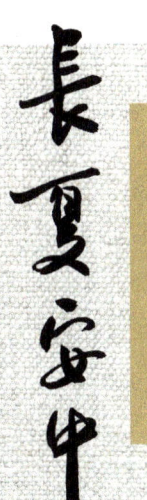

During this transitional season between summer and autumn, the air is humid and dense. The heat is contained and intensified. Fruit rots, and the earth is laden with organic nutrients.

Organ: Spleen-pancreas. Transformation and transportation.

Color: Orange-yellow.

Taste: Sweet.

Foods: Carrot, sweet potato, pumpkin, beet, pear, banana, mango, date, coconut, cinnamon, honey, rice syrup, jams and soups made from ripe fruits.

Autumn

With light winds and a melancholy atmosphere, autumn marks a beginning and an end. A farewell to summer and the start of a new year. A time of reckoning and promise, a time to let go of the past and plan for the future.

Organ: Lungs. Protection and boundaries.

Color: White.

Taste: Spicy-aromatic.

Foods: Horseradish, radish, kohlrabi, onion, leek, garlic, miso soup.

Winter

Winter is a time for slowing down, for introspection and the preservation of body heat. In winter, our ancestors fed on foods collected during summer and autumn. As the days get shorter and the cold sets in, more time is dedicated to meditation, and to appreciating the quiet and stillness.

Organ: Kidneys. Body wisdom. Ancestral energies.

Color: Blue.

Taste: Salty.

Foods: Soy sauce, seaweed, root vegetables, lentils, stews, soups, sea salt.

春荀

IN SPRING WIND
PEACH BLOSSOMS
BEGIN TO COME APART.
DOUBTS DO NOT GROW
BRANCHES AND LEAVES.

ZEN MASTER DOGEN

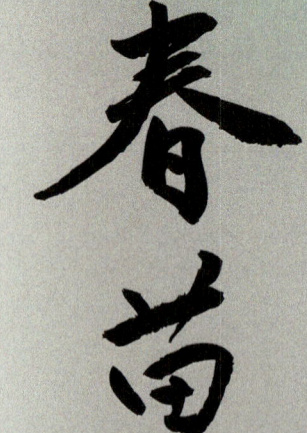

SPRING

Spring

|22-23|	Papaya Plus Smoothie
|24-25|	Japanese Pickles
|26-27|	Vegetable Stuffed Persimmon Fruit Leather in Asian Sauce
|28-29|	Fresh Tabbouleh Salad
|30-31|	Spring Tofu Sandwich
|32-33|	Green Bean and Snow Pea Salad with Purple Cabbage
|34-35|	Spring Pyramid with Artichoke
|36-37|	Spring Soba Noodle Salad
|38-39|	Whole Basmati Rice with Hijiki
|40-43|	Rye and Spelt Flour Sicilian Pizza
|44-45|	Dough-free Asparagus Quiche
|46-47|	Spring Vegetable and Shallot Pie
|48-49|	Carrot Soup with a Hint of Coconut
|50-51|	Juja's Sourdough Bread
|52-53|	Persimmon Sorbet Granola and Maple Syrup Cookies

Papaya Plus Smoothie

Yields 2 liters

1/4 papaya

6 strawberries

1 green apple

3 dates, pitted

2 celery stalks

4 lettuce leaves

4 sprigs mint

5 almonds or walnuts

1 Tbs. coconut oil

4 cups cold water

5 ice cubes

super-food additive
(10 chlorella tablets or
1 tsp. spirulina powder,
1 tsp. ground
cocoa beans or
2 whole cocoa beans)

Rinse fruits and vegetables and dice. Place in a blender, add water and process to a smooth silky consistency. For desired consistency, add or decrease amount of water.

22 | Five Seasons in the Kitchen

Japanese Pickles

Thoroughly rinse vegetables. Cut cucumbers and carrots into rounds. Cut the remaining vegetables into cubes. In a bowl, combine vegetables with garlic, ginger root and dill. In a separate bowl, mix pickling liquid ingredients. Pour over vegetables. Marinate for 1 hour to absorb flavors.

GOOD TO KNOW

Radishes help strengthen the lungs, cleanse the kidneys, neutralize toxins and boost the immune system. This recipe was inspired by the late Irit Muzan, a talented and dear friend.

Yields 1 kg.

2 cucumbers

2 carrots

2 red bell peppers

2 kohlrabi

2 radishes

3 cloves garlic, crushed

2 Tbs. fresh ginger root, grated

Pickling liquid

2 Tbs. soy sauce

2 tsp. sesame oil

1 Tbs. sesame seeds

1 cup dill, chopped

2 cups water

1 Tbs. Umeboshi sauce

1 Tbs. rice vinegar

Vegetable Stuffed Persimmon Fruit Leather
in Asian Paste

Yields 8 rolls

8 10x10 cm. sheets persimmon fruit leather or Nori sheet

1 bunch chives

1 zucchini

1 carrot

1 avocado

1 red bell pepper

1 handful sunflower sprouts

250 gr. assorted mushrooms

1 red onion

mung bean sprouts

1 bunch coriander

Paste

1/2 cup soy sauce

2 Tbs. sesame oil

2 Tbs. lemon juice

1 Tbs. olive oil

1 Thai chili pepper

1/4 cup cashews

Persimmon fruit leather

Rinse and peel 5 persimmons. In a food processor, process into a fully combined spread. Spread in thin layers on Teflex sheets and dry in a food dehydrator for 10 hours at 40°C. Alternatively, buy ready-made leather (available at health food stores).

Paste

Process all sauce ingredients in a food processor until smooth and fully combined.

Rolls

Julienne vegetables. Spread a tablespoon of sauce across the center of each leather sheet. Arrange vegetables on top of sauce. Roll sheets and serve.

GOOD TO KNOW

The Goji berry is a tropical fruit containing a high level of anti-oxidants. Its therapeutic properties include boosting the immune system, fortifying the liver and improving blood flow. The Goji berry is rich in vitamins, iron and 18 amino acids. Its tart flavor and bright red color add a unique taste and freshness to a wide variety of dishes.

Fresh Tabbouleh Salad

Serves 4

1 cup coarsely ground bulgur or quinoa

2 cups arugula (rocket)

2 celery stalks

2 cups parsley, chopped

2 lemons, peeled and chopped

1 lime, peeled and chopped

1 cup Goji berries

1/2 cup mint, chopped

1/4 cup olive oil

1 tsp. coarse Atlantic sea salt

Soak bulgur or quinoa in water for 1 hour. Rinse and dry. Rinse vegetables and chop. Mix all ingredients in a salad bowl. Serve.

29 | Spring

Spring Tofu Sandwich

Serves 1

2 slices sour dough bread (recipe on page 50)

100 gr. tofu

1/4 cup soy sauce

1/2 cup water

1/2 ground black pepper

1 radish

1/4 cup sunflower sprouts

3 sprigs coriander

1 tsp. Indian Pesto (recipe on page 98)

Preheat oven to 180°C. Cut tofu into 1/2 cm. thick slices and arrange on a baking pan. Pour soy sauce and water over tofu. Bake for 15 minutes or until liquids evaporate. Cool and refrigerate. Cut peppers and radish into long, narrow strips. Chop sprouts and coriander. Spread both slices of bread with pesto. Arrange tofu on one slice. Top with vegetables, herbs and the second slice of bread.

GOOD TO KNOW

Tofu is produced from soy beans in the form of a large cheese-like lump. It is used as a substitute for animal protein, and is especially popular in Japanese and Korean monasteries where diets are vegetarian. For maximum nutritional value, it is recommended to use fermented, non-genetically modified tofu. Naturally bland in taste, tofu absorbs the flavors of your choice.

Green Bean and Snow Pea Salad
with Purple Cabbage

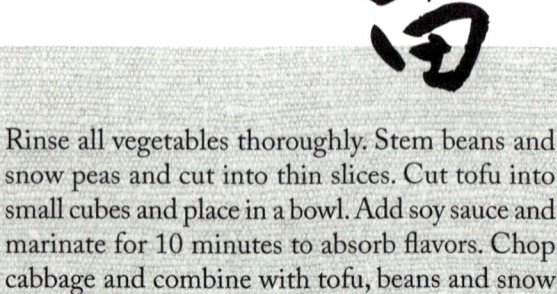

Serves 4

Salad

1 cup green beans

1 cup snow peas

1/4 purple cabbage

4 cherry or sun-dried tomatoes

50 gr. tofu

1 tsp. soy sauce

Dressing

juice from 1 lemon

1 Tbs. olive oil

1 tsp. dried hyssop

1/2 tsp. coarse Atlantic sea salt

Rinse all vegetables thoroughly. Stem beans and snow peas and cut into thin slices. Cut tofu into small cubes and place in a bowl. Add soy sauce and marinate for 10 minutes to absorb flavors. Chop cabbage and combine with tofu, beans and snow peas. Add tomatoes and dressing. Toss and serve.

Oven-Dried Tomatoes: Halve 2 kg. cherry tomatoes. Using a spoon, discard seeds. Arrange tomatoes, skin side down, on a baking pan lined with parchment paper. Sprinkle with salt and a pinch of oregano or thyme. Dry in an oven preheated to 80°C for 8-12 hours. If using a food hydrator, dry at 41°C for 24 hours.

To preserve: arrange tomatoes in a glass jar, cover with olive oil and refrigerate.

GOOD TO KNOW

According to Macrobiotic principles, selenium vegetables such as tomatoes are considered poisonous. Therefore, in this recipe, I substitute fresh tomatoes with sun-dried tomatoes. Though vitamins are lost in the drying process, the tomato's lycopene content – a highly effective anti-oxidant – becomes more readily available. I dry tomatoes in a food dehydrator and preserve them in olive oil. A regular oven will also do the trick.

33 | Spring

Spring Pyramid with Artichoke

Serves 4

Salad

2 artichokes

2 Swiss chard leaves

6 spinach leaves

2 scallions

2 celery stalks

1 avocado

1 red bell pepper

1/4 cup parsley or dill

1 cup pistachios

Dressing

2 tsp. Japanese radish, grated

juice from 1 lemon

juice from 1 orange

1/2 tsp. sesame oil

1 tsp. soy sauce

1/2 tsp. coarse Atlantic sea salt

Cook artichokes in boiling water for 30 minutes. Cool and remove leaves. Using a paring knife or spoon, remove fuzzy fibers from artichoke hearts. Cut hearts into eighths. Thoroughly rinse vegetables. Finely chop Swiss chard, spinach, scallion, red pepper and celery. Peel avocado and dice. Mix vegetables in a bowl, add parsley or dill and pistachios. Put all dressing ingredients in a jar with a tight fitting lid. Shake untill fully combined. Stack vegetables on individual plates to create a pyramid. Pour dressing over vegetables. Serve.

GOOD TO KNOW

Artichokes are rich in dietary fibers that help cleanse the liver, gall bladder and intestines. Fresh or cooked, artichokes make a delicious and healthy snack.

Spring Soba Noodle Salad

Serves 4

1 package (250 gr.) soba noodles gluten free

2 Tbs. sesame oil

2 heads broccoli

1 medium sized cauliflower

1 cup arugula (rocket)

1 cup purple string beans

3 scallions

1 chili pepper

1 Tbs. soy sauce

Garnish

1 Tbs. black sesame seeds

juice from 1 lemon

Cook noodles according to manufacturer's directions; make sure not to overcook. Rinse in cold water, drain, add 1 Tbs. sesame oil and cool. Fill a large bowl with lukewarm water. Add 1 Tbs. salt and soak broccoli, cauliflower and arugula (rocket) for 15 minutes. Remove and drain.

Divide cauliflower and broccoli into florets. Snap tips off beans and cut into quarters. Slice scallions and chili pepper into thin strips. Combine all ingredients in a serving dish. Season with sesame oil and soy sauce. Toss gently. Sprinkle with sesame seeds and drizzle with lemon juice to taste.

GOOD TO KNOW

Soba is Japanese for spelt, or "kasha" in Eastern Europe. Spelt grains' dominant flavor and smell do not appeal to everyone. Soba noodles, on the other hand, do not have a distinctive smell and are great served in warm or cold salads.

Whole Basmati Rice with Hijiki

材料

Serves 4

500 gr. whole Basmati rice

1/4 cup Hijiki

2 Tbs. olive oil

1 onion, finely chopped

1 tsp. curry powder

1 tsp. coarse Atlantic sea salt

4 cups water

Garnish

1 cucumber, finely chopped

1/2 cup dill, rinsed and chopped

Soak rice in water for several hours (to reduce cooking time). Add Hijiki to the water 15 minutes before draining. Drain and rinse until water runs clear. Dry.

Heat olive oil in a wide, deep sauce pan. Add onions and sauté till golden. Add curry, stir and sauté for 1 minute. Add rice, salt and water. Bring to the boil, reduce heat and cook covered for 40 minutes. Drain and arrange rice on a serving dish. Garnish with chopped cucumbers and dill.

GOOD TO KNOW

Basmati rice is a highly satisfying grain rich in soluble fibers that help cleanse the digestive system. Containing vitamin E, the grain's sprouts help retain vitality, delay aging and cleanse tissue cells. Hijiki is rich in iodine and vitamin B12.

Rye and Spelt Flour Sicilian Pizza

材料

Yields 20 individual pizzas

Dough

1 kg. spelt flour

500 gr. rye flour

1 cup olive oil

2 Tbs. dry yeast

or 1 cup of sourdough

2-3 cups lukewarm water

1 tsp. coarse Atlantic sea salt

1 tsp. maple syrup

Vegetable Topping

10 sun-dried tomatoes

12 zucchini, cut into thin rounds

1 eggplant, cut into thin rounds

1 onion, thinly sliced

olive oil

oregano

coarse Atlantic sea salt

3 red bell peppers

100 gr. pumpkin, peeled

Macadamia nut cheese (recipe on page 170)

Tomato Sauce

2 Tbs. olive oil

1 onion, finely chopped

4 cloves garlic, crushed

5 tomatoes, finely chopped

2 cups water

100 gr. tomato paste

1 tsp. coarse Atlantic sea salt

1 tsp. black pepper

fresh oregano, finely chopped

fresh basil, finely chopped

Dough

Combine all ingredients to make a warm, elastic dough. Knead for at least 10 minutes. Cover with a towel and set to rise in a warm place until double in size. Divide dough into ping-pong ball sized portions.

Vegetable topping

Preheat oven to 250°C. Arrange zucchini, eggplant and onion slices on a baking pan lined with parchment paper. Brush with olive oil and sprinkle with oregano and salt. Bake for 15 minutes.

Tomato Sauce

In a pan, sweat onion in olive oil until golden. Add garlic and stir. Add tomatoes and cook until soft. Add water, tomato paste, salt and pepper and cook on low heat for 15 minutes. Add herbs and cook for an additional 15 minutes. Transfer sauce to food processer and process till smooth.

Assemble Pizza

Lower oven heat to 200°C. Roll out balls of dough as thinly as possible. Evenly spread tomato sauce, top with vegetables and Bake for 15 minutes.

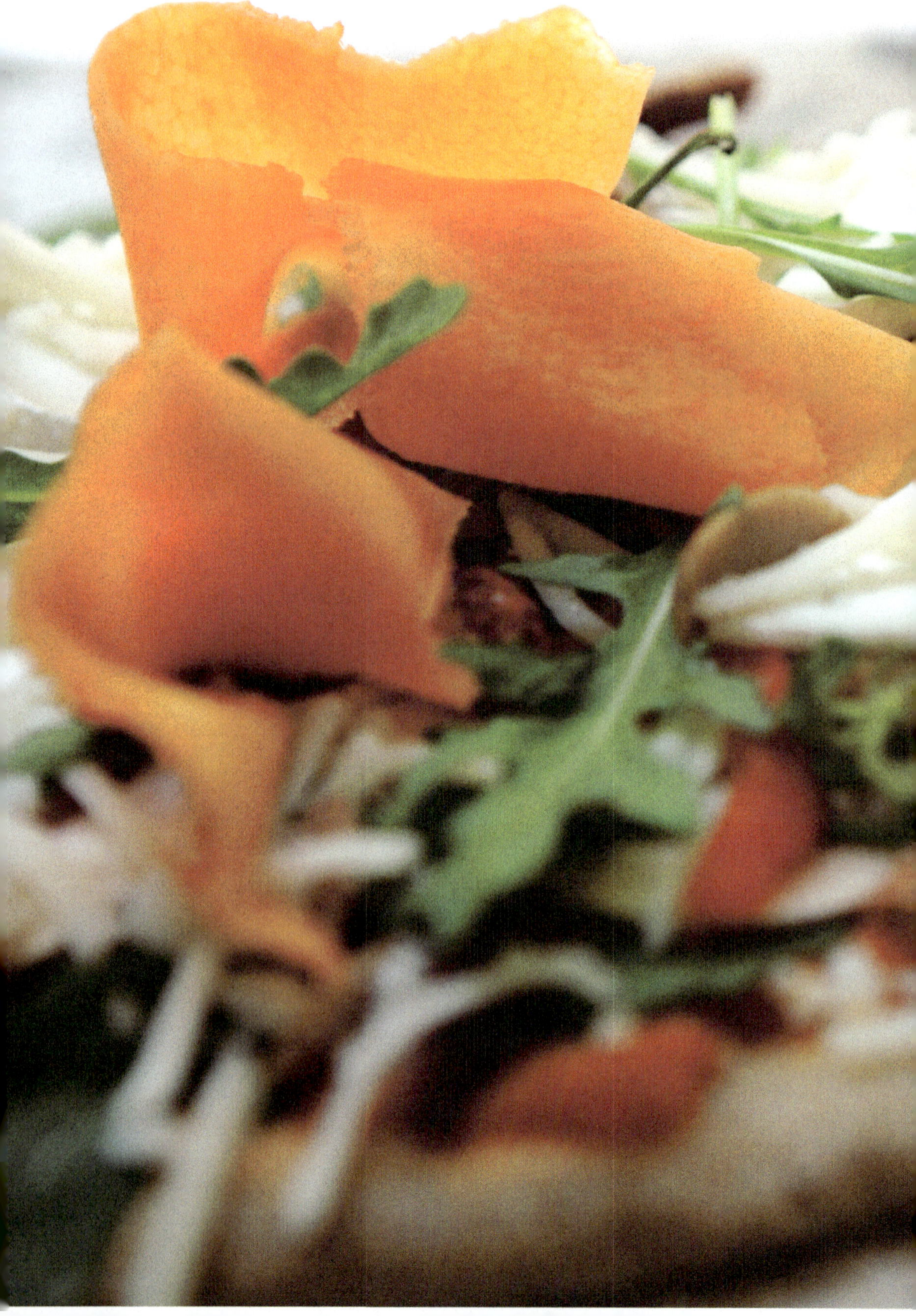

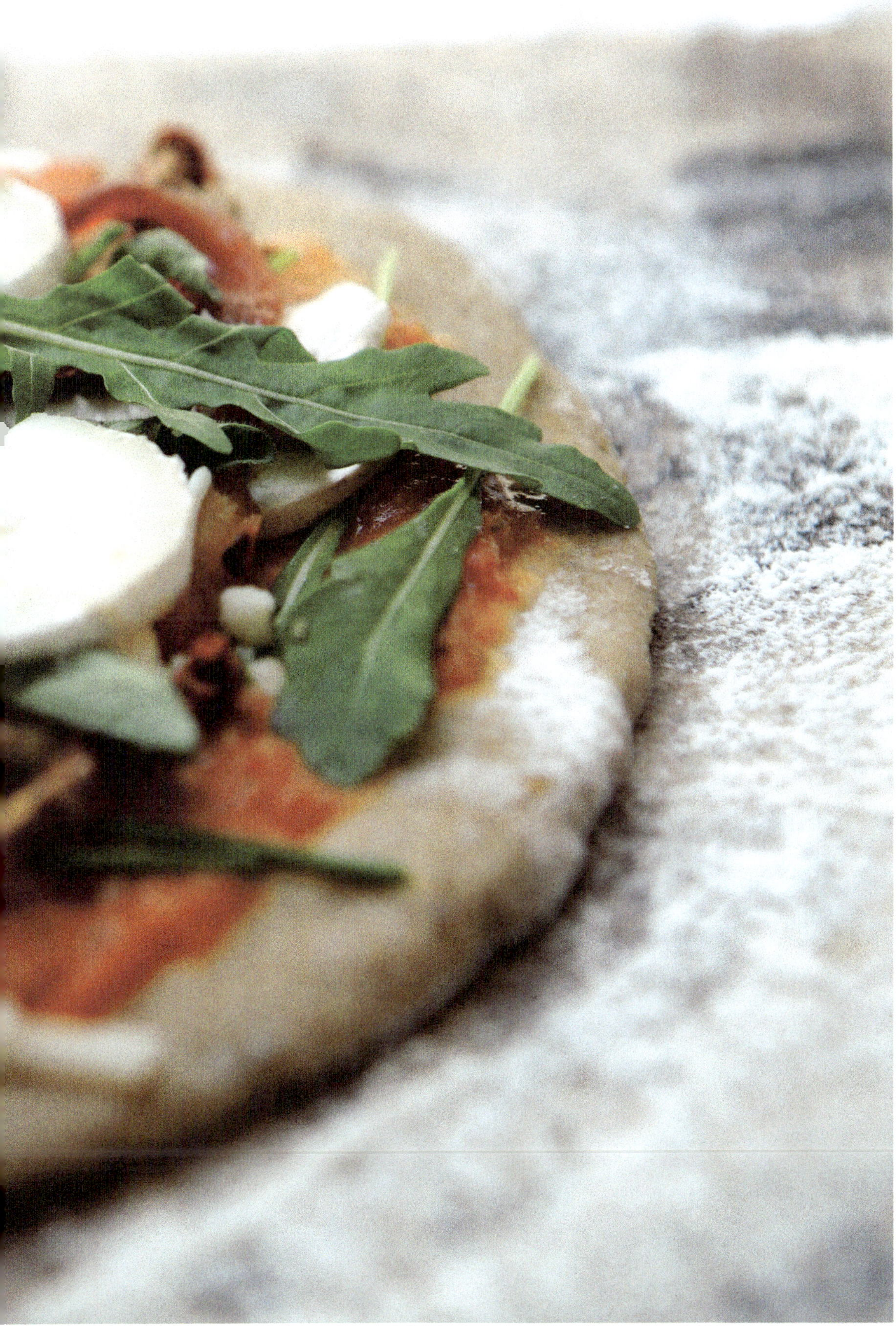

Dough-free Asparagus Quiche

材料

26 cm. pie dish
or 6 individual
6 cm. pie dishes

1 bunch asparagus

2 leeks

1 cup olive oil

10 Kalamata olives, pitted

10 sun-dried tomatoes

1 bunch basil

3 cloves garlic, crushed

2 cups Macadamia nut cheese (recipe on page 170)

salt and pepper

sesame seeds

Preheat oven to 180°C. Scald asparagus in boiling water for 2 minutes. Cut into 4 cm. slices and place in a mixing bowl. Cut leeks into rounds and sweat in 1 Tbs. olive oil in a pan. Add leeks to bowl. Chop olives, tomatoes and basil. Add to bowl with garlic.

In a separate bowl, add olive oil, Macadamia nut cheese, salt and pepper and mix. Pour mixture over vegetables and combine till fully coated. Transfer to pie dish or individual dishes. Sprinkle with sesame seeds. Bake for 20 minutes. Lower heat to 140°C and bake for an additional 25 minutes.

GOOD TO KNOW

Most of us are familiar with exclusive varieties of asparagus sold in supermarkets and vegetable markets. There is however another option—a wild, non-cultivated variety that grows in Israel's natural groves throughout the spring. Similar in shape, but thinner than the cultivated variety, wild asparagus is crispy and can be eaten fresh. Asparagus's dark green color is indicative of its high chlorophyll content that is exceptionally beneficial for cleansing the liver and dissolving kidney stones.

Spring Vegetable and Shallot Pie

材料

26 cm. pie dish or
6 individual 6 cm.
pie dishes

Dough

2 cups spelt flour

1/2 cup olive oil

1/2 cup cashews, chopped

1/2 cup water

1 tsp. lemon juice

Filling

3 Tbs. olive oil

2 shallots, chopped

4 King Oyster mushrooms, chopped

1 head broccoli

2 cups spinach

1 cup olive oil

500 gr. Macadamia nut cheese
(recipe on page 170)

5 basil leaves

3 cloves garlic, crushed

salt and pepper

Dough

Mix spelt flour and olive oil until fully incorporated. Add cashews, water and lemon juice and mix. If necessary, add water to make a smooth dough. Cover and refrigerate for 30 minutes.

Filling

Heat olive oil in a wide pan. Sweat shallots. Add mushrooms and sweat for 5 minutes. Scald broccoli in boiling water for 2 minutes and cut into thin slices. In a bowl, mix olive oil, Macadamia nut cheese, basil, garlic and spices. Combine with mushrooms and broccoli.

Preheat oven to 180°C. Roll out the dough and place in the pie dish, pressing it evenly into the bottom and sides. Perforate dough with a fork. Pour in filling. Bake for 20 minutes. Reduce heat to 140°C and bake for an additional 25 minutes.

47 | Spring

Carrot Soup with a Hint of Coconut

材料

Serves 6

6 carrots

4 small parsley roots or 1 large, quarted

1 celery root, peeled

2 leeks

1 onion

3 cloves garlic

1 celery stalk

3 Tbs. coconut oil

1 tsp. black pepper

1 Tbs. coarse Atlantic sea salt

3 liters water

Garnish

1 Tbs. black sesame seeds

1/4 cup broccoli or mung bean sprouts

Rinse carrots and parsley roots thoroughly (if organic, no need to peel). Cube carrots, parsley and celery roots. Cut leeks and onion into rounds. In a large pot, sweat leeks and onions in coconut oil. Add carrots, roots, spices and 3 liters water. Bring to the boil, reduce heat and simmer for 1 hour. Using a hand blender, puree soup until smooth and silky. Pour into soup bowls. Garnish with sesame seeds and sprouts. Serve.

GOOD TO KNOW

Sprouts are a healthy substitute for croutons. They contain enzymes that help cleanse the body's cells. Lentils and seeds can be easily sprouted at home using a colander, canvas sprouting bag, glass jar, tiered or electric sprouter. I recommend starting out with legumes such as mung beans or lentils that are easy to sprout.

Joja's Sourdough Bread

Sourdough Starter

10 raisins

1 cup water

4 cups lukewarm water

5 cups spelt flour

Bread

2 loaf pans

1 cup starter

1 kg. spelt flour

1 Tbs. salt

1/4 cup olive oil

1 1/2 liters lukewarm water

Optional Additions

1 cup oats, raisins, prunes, olives

Sourdough Starter

1. Soak raisins in 1 cup water for 8 hours at room temperature. In a bowl, combine soaking liquid and 1 cup flour. Transfer to a jar and cover with cheesecloth. Keep at room temperature for 1 day.

2. On the second day, add 1 cup each of flour and water to the starer jar, once a day for 3 days. On the fourth day your sourdough starter is ready to use. Best kept refregerated.

3. Your starter needs weekly "feeding" by adding a cup each of flower and water or by replacing the amount of starter used for baking. Make sure to have at least 2 cups starter in your fridge at all times.

Bread

Lightly grease loaf pans with olive oil. Mix all ingredients including starter. Pour into pans, filling up to 3/4 from top. Using a wet spoon or spatula, smooth surface. Cover with a towel and let rise in a warm place for 5-6 hours, depending on the season.

Heat oven to 250°C. Bake 10 minutes, reduce heat to 180°C and bake for an additional hour or when loaf sounds hollow when tapping.

Remove loaves from pans, cover with a towel and cool on a rack.

50 | Five Seasons in the Kitchen

GOOD TO KNOW

Sourdough is like a living organism, in need of constant care and nutrition. As a primary ingredient that is traditionally passed on from one baker to another, sourdough has evolved into many varieties, each of which carries a unique personal story.

My sourdough starter originated in a Korean monastery in Hungary. While visiting there, I was served wonderfully flavored bread, and so I asked the cook, a Polish nun named Bulchawa Han Zanim, for the recipe. She gladly shared the recipe and a portion of her starter with me. This particular starter, she explained, was given to her by her Polish friend Joja, who had received it from a friend of hers.

51 | Spring

Persimmon Sorbet | Granola and Maple Syrup Cookies

材料

Persimmon Sorbet

Yields 500 ml.

1 kg. ripe persimmons

juice from 4 oranges

1 Tbs. coconut oil

1/4 cup maple syrup

1/2 cup pecans

Granola and Maple Syrup Cookies

Yields 10-20 cookies

2 cups granola

1/4 cup coconut oil

3/4 cup spelt flour

1/2 cup maple syrup

2 Tbs. flax seeds, soaked

Optional

zest from 1/4 lemon

shredded coconut

sugar-free, store bought granola with dried fruit

Sorbet

Combine all ingredients in a blender until fully incorporated and smooth. Pour mixture into a divided silicon mold of your choice (triangles, hearts, etc.). Freeze. Sorbet can be served with a granola cookie (see recipe below), and garnished with bittersweet chocolate shavings.

Cookies

Preheat oven to 180°C. Combine and mix all ingredients into a sticky batter (do not add flour). Using a tablespoon, scoop portions onto a baking pan lined with parchment paper. No need to flatten, the batter will spread while baking. Bake for 15 minutes until golden, or for 24 hours in a food dehydrator at 41°C.

GOOD TO KNOW

Persimmons are rich in nutritional fibers, vitamin A, beta-carotene and anti-oxidants. In Chinese medicine, persimmons and other orange fruits and vegetables, are considered especially effective in boosting the digestive system. This sorbet can be made with other fruits that ripen in the spring, preferably those with dense textures such as mango, papaya, banana and even avocado.

When preparing pastries, cakes and cookies, I recommend substituting sugar with natural sweeteners. I prefer organic maple syrup, rice malt, molasses, honey or sugar-free date honey.

夏神

ALL THIS RIPENESS,
IN OUR BEDS, FIGS,
DATES,
WATERMELON,
GRAPES,
MULBERRIES.
SUMMER LOVE.

SEFI RACHLEVSKI

SUMMER

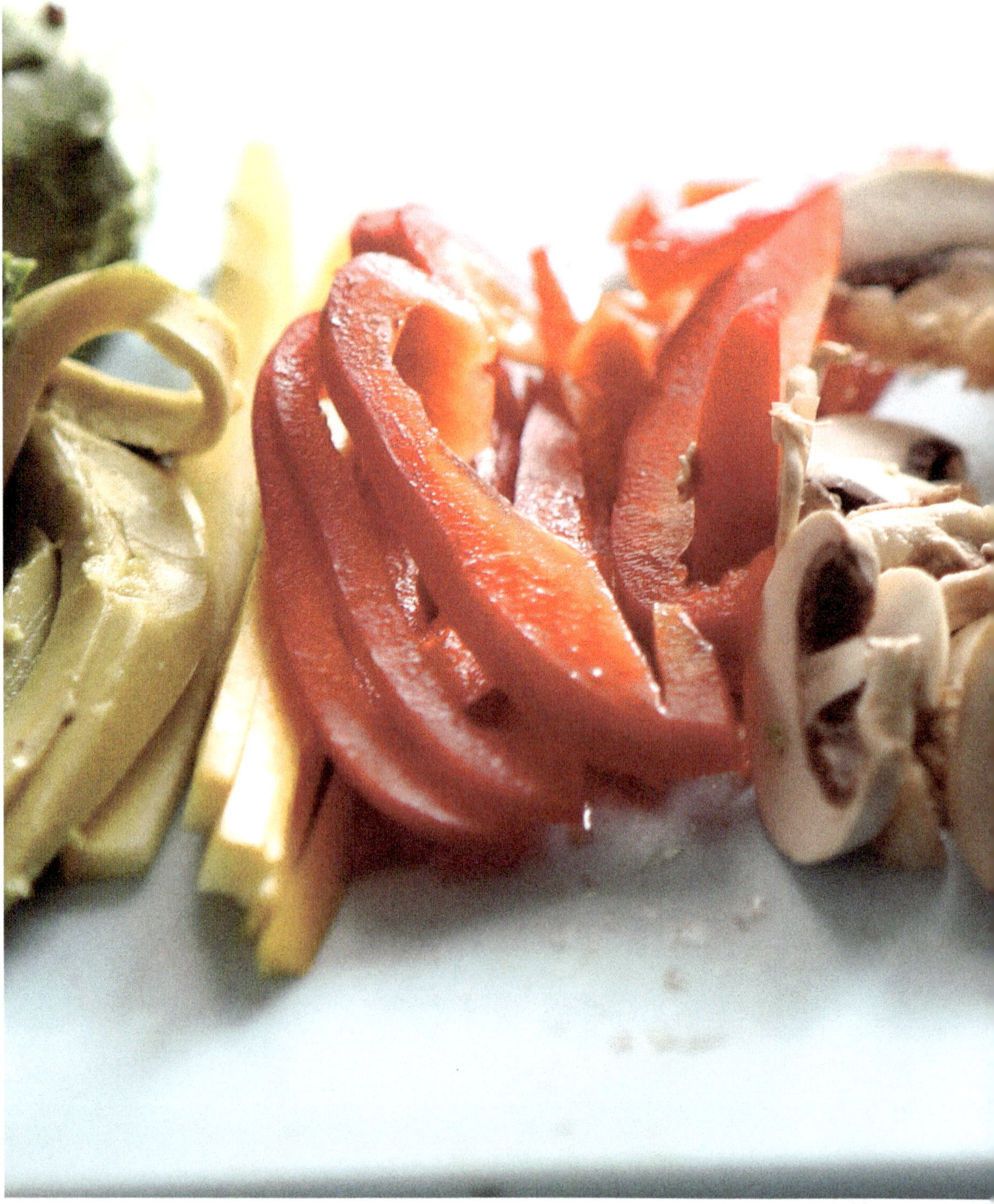

目錄

Summer

	58-59		Pomegranate and Lime Drink
	60-61		Endive Boats with Feta or Macadamia Nuts
	62-63		Asparagus Wrapped in Seaweed with Tofu and Lemon Crumbs
	64-65		Beet Pillows Stuffed with Almond-Sprout Spread
	66		Roasted Eggplant in Tahini Paste
	67		Baked Cauliflower
	68-69		Baked Vegetable Chips
	70-71		Three Way Toastini
	72		Green Salad with Mustard Miso Dressing
	73		Asian Papaya Salad
	76-77		Black Rice Noodles and Kohlrabi
	78-79		Squash Flowers Stuffed with Mushrooms, Asparagus and Pine Nuts
	80-83		Shosh Caviat's Hummus and Broad Bean Spread
	84-85		Baked Falafel
	86-87		Lady Fingers
	88-89		Nut Ice Cream Nuggets

57 | Summer

58 | Five Seasons in the Kitchen

Pomegranate and Lime Drink

材料

Yields 2 cups

2 pomegranates
or 2 tsp. natural
pomegranate syrup

2 kobo (tropical fruit)

1 lime

2 pears

1 cup mint leaves

1 tsp. hemp oil

Juice pomegranates into clear juice. Peel lime and kobo. Thoroughly rinse mint leaves and pears. In a heavy duty juicer, process pears and mint into a clear, fiber-free juice. Mix with pomegranate juice and hemp oil.

GOOD TO KNOW

Hemp oil is produced from the part of cannabis seeds that do not contain significant amounts of the psychoactive element tetrahydrocannabinol (THC). The seeds contain a high concentration (80%) of fatty acids. Hemp oil is rich in anti-oxidants, helps reduce risks for cancer and heart diseases, boosts energy and contributes to weight loss. It is recommended to consume hemp oil daily.

ENDIVE BOATS STUFFED WITH MACADAMIA FETA

Serves 8

12 endives, (preferably with wide leaves)

Stuffing

100 gr. Macadamia nuts

6 Kalamata olives, pitted

4 sun-dried tomatoes

1/4 cup chopped coriander

water (as needed)

Garnish

1/4 cup sesame seeds

8 basil leaves

8 beet juliennes

1 Tbs. olive oil

Rinse endive thoroughly. Gently separate leaves. In a food processor, combine all stuffing ingredients into a coarse, thick paste. Add water as needed. Form stuffing into small balls using a Parisian spoon or tablespoon. Roll balls in sesame seeds. Place a basil leaf in each endive "boat" followed by a ball of stuffing. Garnish with beet juliennes. Drizzle with olive oil (optional).

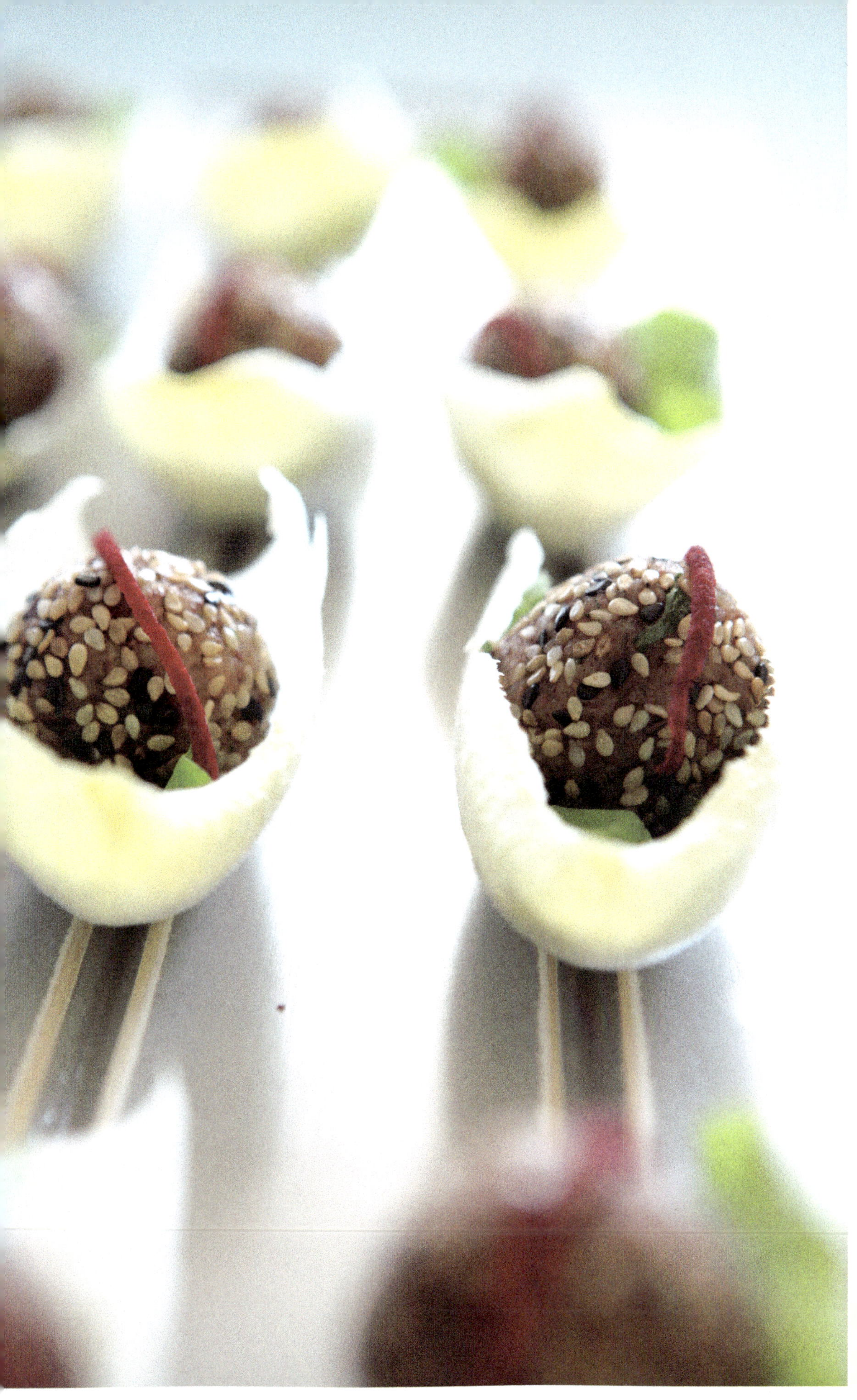

ASPARAGUS WRAPPED IN SEAWEED
WITH TOFU AND LEMON CRUMBS

Steam asparagus in bamboo steamer for exactly 3 minutes or blanch in boiling water. Roast almonds in a hot skillet with a drizzle of olive oil and salt, or in a food hydrator at 41°C for 5 hours. Dice tofu and marinate in soy sauce for 10 minutes. Place asparagus on a serving dish. Wrap each asparagus sprig with a slice of Nori. Arrange tofu cubes on top of asparagus and dress with lemon juice and olive oil. Sprinkle with almonds, and drizzle with tahini. Garnish with radish sprouts. Serve immediately.

材料

Serves 4-6

1 bunch asparagus

100 gr. peeled almonds

200 gr. tofu

2 Tbs. soy sauce

1 Nori sheet,
cut into thin slices

juice from 1 lemon

1/4 cup olive oil

3 Tbs. tahini paste

1 cup radish sprouts

1 liter water

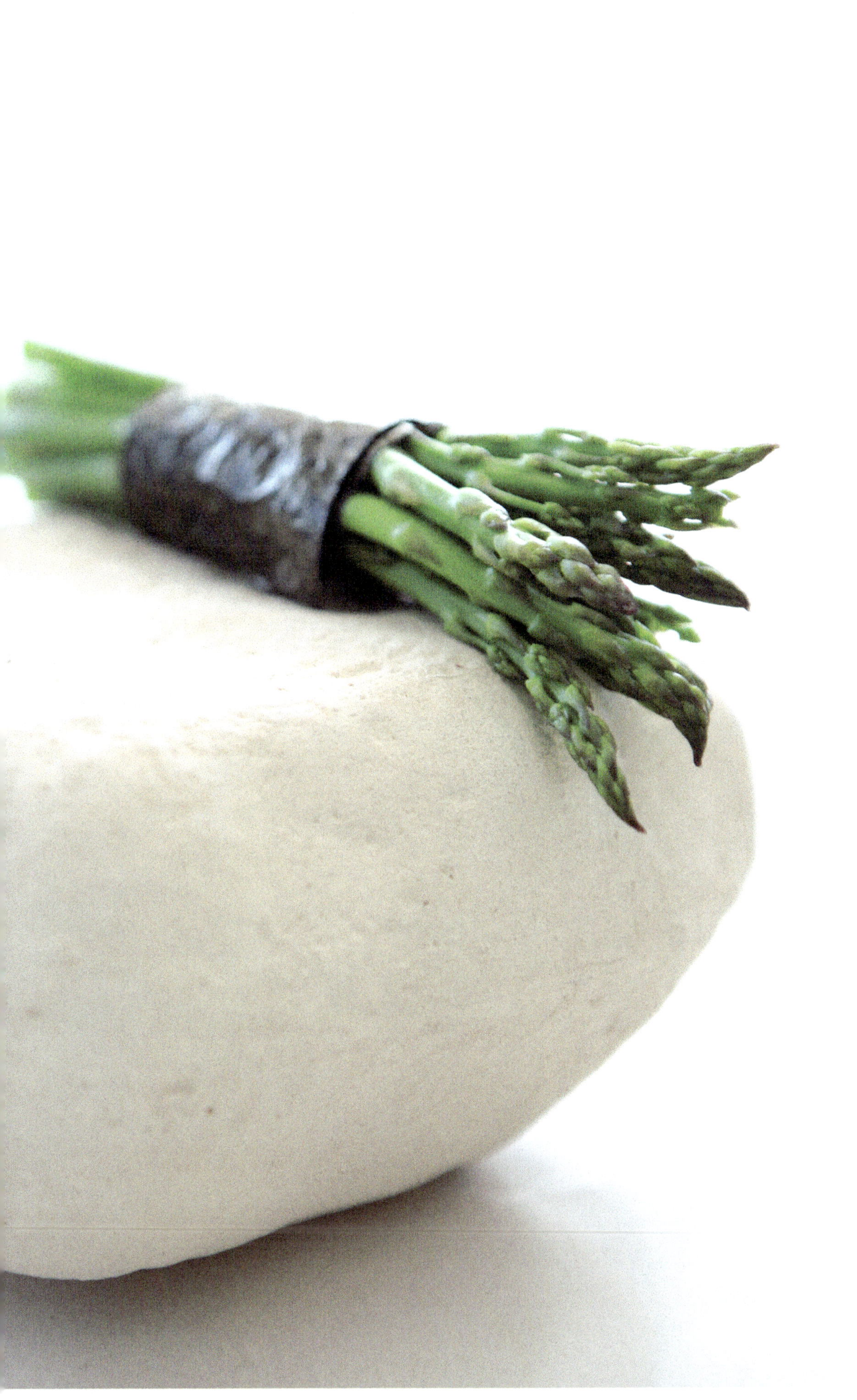

Beet Pillows Stuffed
with Almond-Sprout Spread

Serves 4

2 large beets

1 bunch parsley

handful broccoli sprouts

Stuffing

1 cup almonds, soaked in lukewarm water for 12 hours

1 Tbs. tahini paste

1/4 ginger root

1 jalapeño pepper

2 cloves garlic

juice from 1/2 a lemon

1 Tbs. Umeboshi sauce

1/2 cup water

1/2 tsp. black pepper

To serve

1 Tbs. olive oil

1 Tbs. lemon juice

Peel beets. Cut into thin slices and soak in water for 1 hour. Chop parsley. In a food processor, process all stuffing ingredients for 3 minutes into a smooth spread.

Arrange beet slices on a serving dish. Place 1 tsp. almond spread onto half the amount of slices. Garnish with chopped parsley, cover with a beet slice and repeat. In a small bowl, mix olive oil and lemon juice. Pour over beets. Garnish with broccoli sprouts.

GOOD TO KNOW

Beets can be eaten cooked or raw. Raw beets should be soaked in a pickling solution such as brine or lemon juice. This recipe is a vegan variation on ravioli. To slice beets, I recommend using a mandolin set at desired thickness.

Roasted Eggplant in Tahini Paste

GOOD TO KNOW

Eggplants are acidic, so I recommend consuming small quantities as appetizers or side dishes.

Roast eggplant on an open fire (BBQ, grill or stove) until scorched on all sides. Cool. Remove skin, leaving cap and stem attached. In a small bowl, mix ginger, garlic, soy sauce and pepper. Place eggplant on a serving dish. Pour dressing over eggplant, drizzle with tahini paste and sprinkle with sesame.

Serves 1-2

1 eggplant

1/2 ginger root, grated

2 cloves garlic, grated

2 tsp. soy sauce

1/2 tsp. black pepper

2 tsp. tahini paste

2 tsp. sesame seeds

Tahini paste is available in multiple varieties. I recommend using Ethiopian tahini, made from sprouted, whole organic sesame in a cold press process. This tahini is dark in color, and has a bitter sweet taste developed through the sprouting of seeds. Sprouting also accounts for high levels of enzymes and oxalic acid that enhance body cells' absorption of calcium and other vital minerals.

BAKED CAULIFLOWER

Soak cauliflower in a bowl of salt water for 1 hour. Drain and brush with olive oil. Sprinkle with salt and herbs. Preheat oven at 100°C. Wrap cauliflower in parchment paper and bake for 20 minutes. Remove parchment paper, turn cauliflower over and bake for an additional 20 minutes.

材料

Serves 4

1 whole cauliflower

1 Tbs. olive oil

1 tsp. coarse Atlantic sea salt

Herbs to taste (thyme, oregano, rosemary)

GOOD TO KNOW

Soaking vegetables in salt water (or a water-vinegar solution) helps get rid of insects

Baked Vegetable Chips

Rinse vegetables thoroughly. Dry and cut into thin slices using a mandolin or vegetable peeler.

Sweet Potato Chips

Arrange slices on a flat baking pan. Cover with water, add apple vinegar and marinate for 15 minutes. Drain. Brush with olive oil and sprinkle with sea salt and chili powder. See baking instructions below.

Beet Chips

Arrange slices on baking pan lined with parchment paper or on a food dehydrator pan lined with a sheet of non stick Teflex. Brush with olive oil and sprinkle with salt. See baking instructions below.

Zucchini Chips

Arrange slices on a flat baking pan lined with parchment paper or a food dehydrator pan lined with a sheet of non stick Teflex. Brush with olive oil and sprinkle with salt and Italian herbs. See baking instructions below.

Baking

Food dehydrator: dry for 4 hours on Teflex. Remove Teflex. Turn chips over and dry for an additional 6-8 hours.

Oven: preheat oven at 100°C. Bake for 1 hour. Turn chips over and bake for an additional hour.

材料

Yields 300 gr.

1 beet

1 sweet potato

3 zucchini

1 Tbs. olive oil

2 Tbs. water

1 tsp. apple vinegar

1 Tbs. coarse Atlantic sea salt

1/2 tsp. chili powder

1 tsp. mixed Italian herbs (oregano, thyme, basil)

Three Way Toastini

材料

Yields 6

6 slices rye bread

1 Tbs. Indian Pesto
(recipe on pg 98)

1 Tbs. Sun-dried Tomato,
Walnuts and
Ginger Spread
(recipe on pg 98)

1 Tbs. Sprouted Lentil
and Walnut Spread
(recipe on pg 98)

6 slices tofu, marinated
in soy sauce for
5 minutes

3 sun-dried tomatoes,
thinly sliced

3 Champignon
mushrooms,
thinly sliced

Garnish

1 cucumber, diced

1/2 cup dill, chopped

Preheat oven to 200°C. (roast or grill setting). Spread each slice of bread with one of the spreads. Top with tofu, tomatoes and mushrooms. Arrange on a baking pan lined with parchment paper. Grill for 15 minutes.

GOOD TO KNOW

According to Chinese medicine, scorched-grilled flavors are characteristic of summer. Toastini is an excellent appetizer or light meal. The tofu can be substituted with Macadamia nut cheese (see recipe on page 170) or any other variety of vegan cheese.

71 | Summer

Green Salad with Mustard Miso Dressing

Rinse spinach and lettuce thoroughly. Dry in a lettuce spinner. Gently tear leaves, and arrange in a salad bowl. Combine dressing ingredients, and pour over leaves before serving. Garnish with edible flowers such as pansies.

Serves 4

1 bunch assorted lettuce

1 bunch Turkish spinach

Dressing

1 Tbs. light miso

1 tsp. mustard

1/2 tsp. black pepper

1 Tbs. olive oil

juice from 1 lemon

Asian Papaya Salad

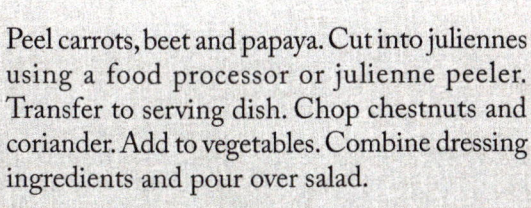

Peel carrots, beet and papaya. Cut into juliennes using a food processor or julienne peeler. Transfer to serving dish. Chop chestnuts and coriander. Add to vegetables. Combine dressing ingredients and pour over salad.

材料

Serves 4

Salad

2 carrots

1 beet

1 green papaya

1 cup chestnuts, peeled

1/2 cup coriander leaves

Dressing

juice from 1 lime

1 tsp. chili oil

1 tsp. coarse Atlantic sea salt

1 tsp. sesame oil

1 tsp. Nigella seed oil

GOOD TO KNOW

I was first introduced to papaya salad by a Thai woman named Nowi. Nowi worked in my kitchen for two years. The original recipe is made with green papaya and cherry tomatoes only, and the dressing is based on fish sauce. In this version, I substitute fish sauce with a combination of sesame and Nigella oils.

73 | Summer

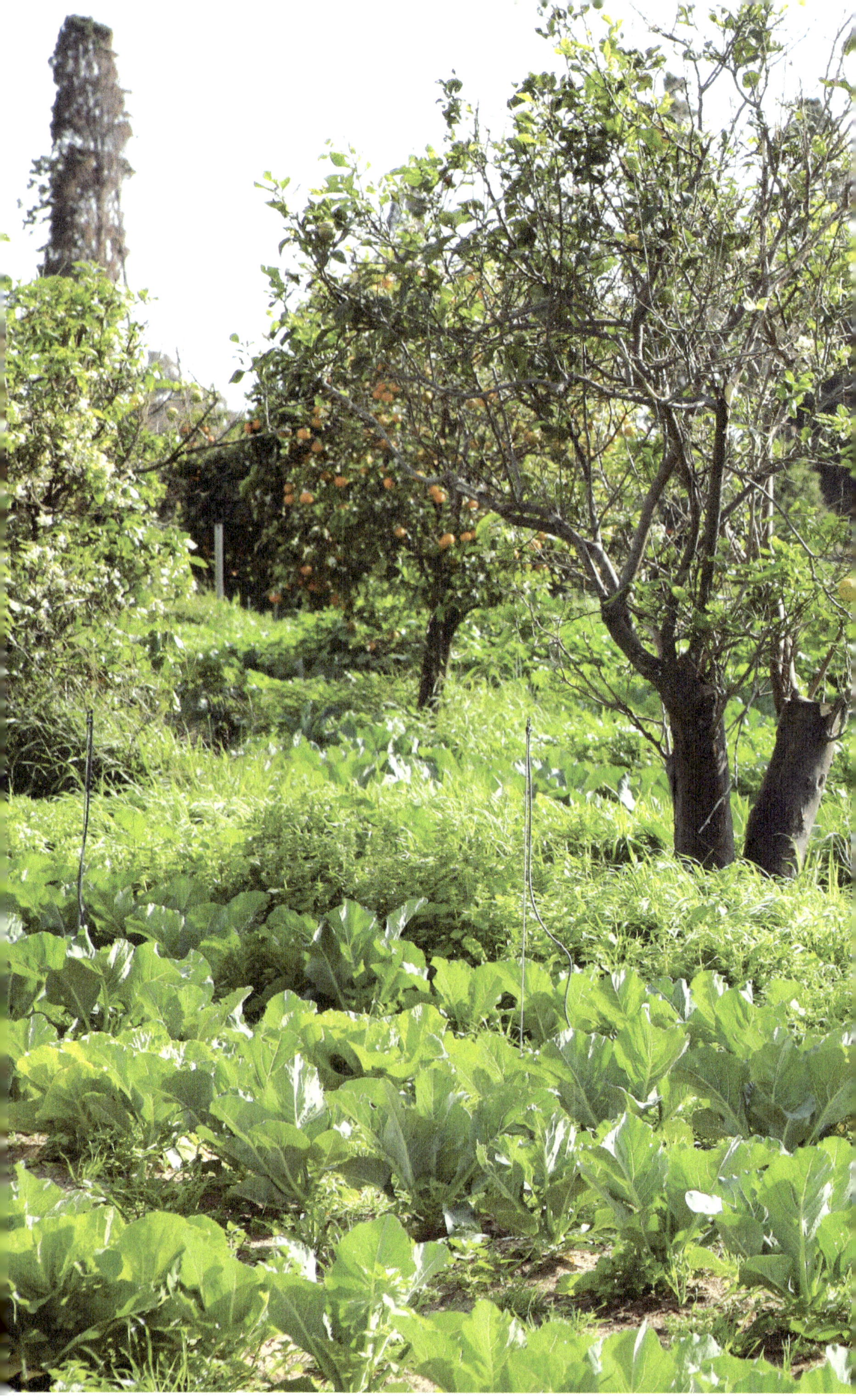

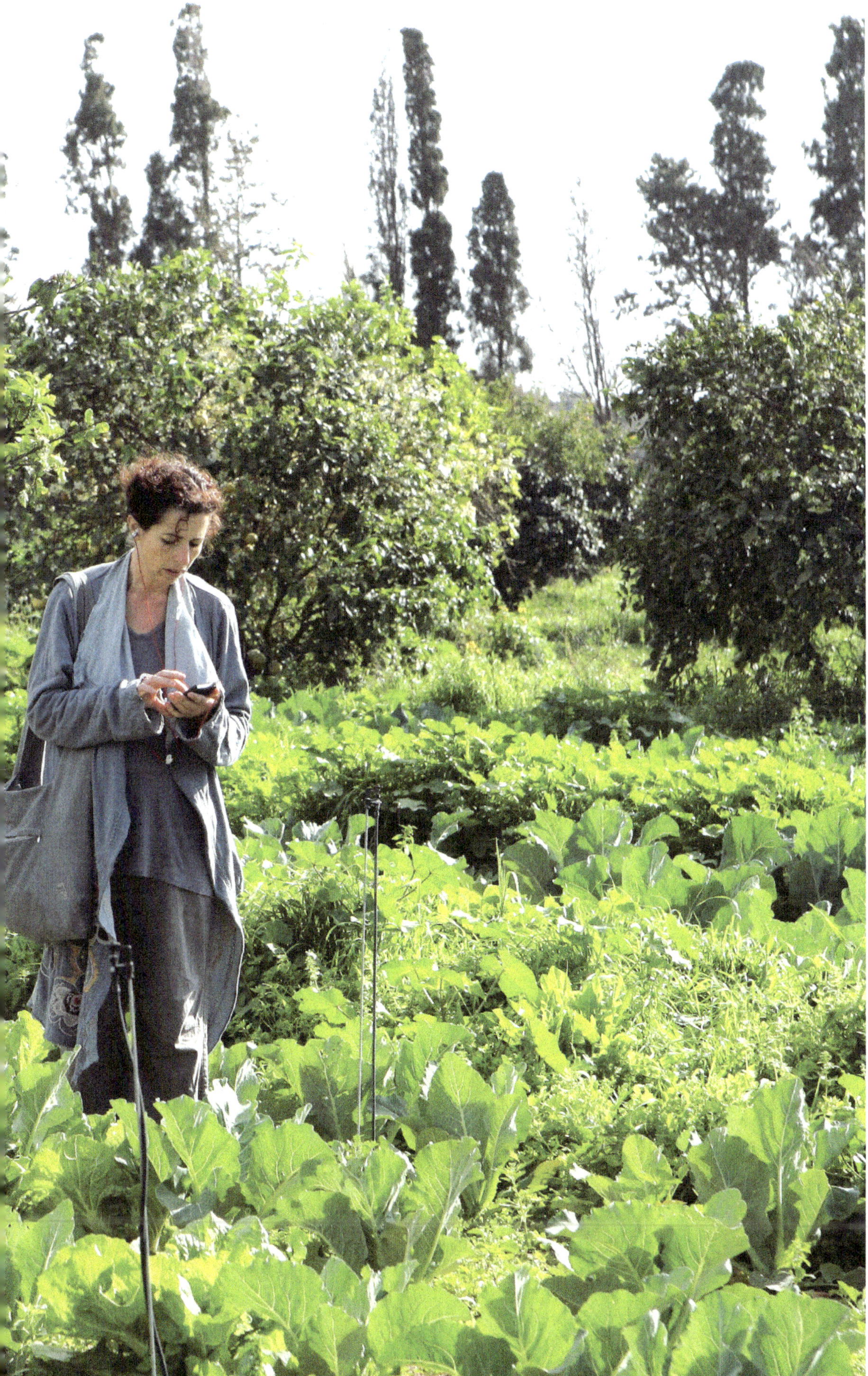

Black Rice Noodles and Kohlrabi

Serves 4

1 package (250 gr.) black rice noodles

2 kohlrabi

2 scallions

1 cup mixed herbs: coriander, parsley, dill

1 tsp. coarse Atlantic sea salt

Dressing

1 piece ginger root (to taste)

1 Tbs. soy sauce

juice from 1 lemon

1 Tbs. sesame oil

1 tsp. black pepper

Cook rice noodles according to manufacturer's instructions. Drain, rinse and cool. Cut scallions into rounds. Soak herbs in lukewarm water with 1 tsp. salt for 15 minutes. Rinse, dry and chop. Peel kohlrabi and julienne using julienne knife or food processor. In a mixing bowl, combine noodles, kohlrabi, scallions and herbs. Grate ginger into a separate bowl. Add soy sauce, sesame oil, lemon juice and pepper. Whisk until fully combined. Pour over noodles, mix and serve.

GOOD TO KNOW

Black rice noodles are made from black rice flour, and are commonly used in Asian cuisine. Because they do not contain gluten (found in wheat flour), rice noodles are a delicious solution for people with celiac disease or sensitive to gluten.

Squash Flowers Stuffed
with Mushrooms, Asparagus and Pine Nuts

Preheat oven to 180°C. In a pan, sauté red onion in 1 tsp. olive oil until browned. Chop mushrooms and asparagus. Add to pan with garlic and herbs and sauté for 5 minutes. Cool. Roast pine nuts in a pan or in a food dehydrator for 3 hours. Cool and add to mushroom mixture with Macadamia nut cheese and chives. Open squash flowers gently, discard pollen and stuff with vegetable stuffing. Pinch and twist flowers to close hermetically. Roll flowers in batter. Place on a baking pan lined with parchment paper and bake for 30 minutes.

Dressing

Chop onions and sauté in olive oil until browned. Dice tomatoes. Add to onions with garlic and seasonings. Sauté for 15 minutes. Add 1/2 cup water and simmer for an additional 10 minutes. Transfer to food processor and process till fully combined. Pour over stuffed flowers. Top with Macadamia nut cheese. Serve.

Serves 4

1 red onion, chopped

12 fresh squash flowers

250 gr. assorted mushrooms

1/2 bunch asparagus

2 cloves garlic

50 gr. pine nuts

1 cup Macadamia nut cheese (recipe on pg 170)

2 Tbs. chives, chopped

1 Tbs. olive oil

1/2 tsp. black pepper

1 tsp. coarse Atlantic sea salt

1/4 cup fresh oregano

Batter

1 cup spelt bread crumbs

1 cup coconut oil

Dressing

1 onion

4 tomatoes

1 clove garlic

1 tsp. oregano

1 tsp. coarse Atlantic sea salt

GOOD TO KNOW

Squash flowers are not only beautiful to look at, they're considered the ultimate gourmet ingredient. It's no wonder world renown chefs celebrate their arrival in the autumn by adding them to a wide variety of recipes. Stuffed with vegetables, squash flowers are undoubtedly one of the most delicious delicacies imaginable.

Shosh Caviat's Hummus and Broad Bean Special

材料

Serves 10

Hummus Spread

500 gr. dry chickpeas

1 tsp. cumin

100 gr. tahini paste

juice from 2 lemons

2 tsp. olive oil

1 tsp. coarse Atlantic sea salt

4-6 cloves garlic

water, as needed (reserve chickpea cooking liquid)

Broad Bean Stew

500 gr. dry broad beans

juice from 2 lemons

2 onions, chopped

4 cloves garlic, chopped

4 Tbs. olive oil

1 tsp. salt

1 tsp. black pepper

1 tsp. chili pepper

2 liters water

Hummus Spread

Soak chickpeas in water for 8 hours. Rinse thoroughly, drain and leave in colander for 8 hours until they begin to sprout. Transfer sprouted chickpeas to a pressure cooker. Add water to cover (approx. 1 cm. above chickpeas). Cook for 1 hour. If using a regular pot, cook for 2 hours.

Drain chickpeas. Reserve liquid. In a food processor, process chickpeas while gradually adding tahini paste, juice from one lemon and garlic. Season with salt, cumin and olive oil. Process for approximately 15 minutes to desired consistency. Texture depends on the amount of time processed, while thickness is determined by the amount of cooking liquids added.

Broad Bean Stew

Soak beans in water for 8 hours. Cook in a pressure cooker for 1 hour, or in a regular pot for 1 1/2 hours until beans are soft. In a pan, sweat onions in 1 tsp. olive oil until golden. Add garlic and stir. Add beans, lemon juice and the remaining olive oil. Season with salt and pepper. Stir until fully combined.

To Serve

Spread hummus evenly on a flat plate. Add 2 Tbs. broad bean mixture. Sprinkle with sweet paprika and dried hyssop (optional) and drizzle with olive oil. Serve with lemon juice and zhug (hot pepper paste).

GOOD TO KNOW

Home-made hummus spread is easy to make. Unlike store bought hummus, it does not contain preservatives and so does not keep for long. I recommend making small quantities at a time.

On a personal note: Shosh Caviat was my close friend for over thirty years. From the time I left my parents' house and moved into my own home, until she passed away, she treated me like a daughter. She taught me the basics of cooking, shared many tips for working in the kitchen, but most importantly, Shosh taught me not to be afraid. On Saturdays her home was filled with family and friends who gathered around her table to savor an abundance of homemade salads. Shosh's guests especially enjoyed dipping fresh yeman pita bread in hummus and broad bean stew, accompanied by a fresh green leaf and onion salad.

GOOD TO KNOW

I was first introduced to this recipe at the "Pure Food and Wine" restaurant in New York City. Based on sprouted lentils, it is a variation on Samara's (a visionary leader of the raw food school) original version.

BAKED FALAFEL

Soak lentils in water for 8 hours. Rinse and place in a colander or sprouting bag for 24 hours. Rinse with water every 2 hours - lentils will produce tiny green sprouts. Transfer to a food processor, add remaining falafel ingredients and process till fully combined. Form balls from mixture. Arrange on a baking pan lined with parchment paper. Press each ball gently. Bake in an oven preheated to 180°C for 20 minutes, or in a food dehydrator at 40°C for 8-10 hours.

Dressing

Process all ingredients in a food processor until fully combined and smooth. Serve aside falafel balls. Optional: serve with pita bread.

Yields 25 balls

Falafel Mixture

1 cup sprouted green lentils

1 cup almonds, soaked in water for 12 hours

1 cup cashews, soaked in water for 12 hours

1/2 cup ground fresh flax seed

1/4 cup sesame seeds

1 cup chopped parsley

1/4 tsp. coarse Atlantic sea salt

1 Tbs. lemon juice

3 cloves garlic

1 tsp. cumin

2 Tbs. olive oil

1 Tbs. water (or more)

Dressing

4 Tbs. tahini paste

2 tomatoes

1 bunch parsley

juice from 1 lemon

1 tsp. coarse Atlantic sea salt

LADY FINGERS

材料

Serves 4

500 gr. Sambal Asian okra

1 large onion

6 cloves garlic

6 tomatoes

1 tsp. coarsely ground black pepper

1 tsp. turmeric

1 1/2 Tbs. coarse Atlantic sea salt

1 Tbs. coconut oil

Stem and rinse okra. Place on paper towel and dry in the sun for 30 minutes. Chop onion, garlic and tomatoes. In a wok or deep pan, stir fry onion with coconut oil until browned. Add tomatoes, garlic and spices. Stir fry for 5 minutes. Add okra and bring to the boil. Cover partially, lower flame and simmer for 1 hour.

Serve on a bed of whole rice, quinoa or pearl barley.

On one of my visits to my dear friend Nadav, my personal organic farmer from Givat Olga, he introduced me to an exceptionally long and delicious variety of okra grown by the Thai farmers working on the farm. Until then, I had no idea just how tasty raw okra can be.

GOOD TO KNOW

Okra is available throughout the summer. There are numerous types of okra, the most common of which is the small (2-3 cm. long) variety. The mucilage found in okra protects the intestines. Okra also helps balance sugar levels.

NUT ICE CREAM NUGGETS

Base

In a food processor, coarsely ground all ingredients. Press mixture into the bottom of the pie dish. The base should be about 1 cm. high and even.

Cream Filling

In a blender, blend all filling ingredients until smooth. Pour filling onto base. Freeze for 3 hours to stabilize. Cut pie into small nuggets. Serve.

26 cm. pie dish

Base

3 cups assorted nuts (Macadamia, Brazil, walnut, pecan, almonds)

20 dates, pitted

1/2 cup coconut oil

Cream Filling

juice and zest from 1 lemon

2 cups cashews, soaked in water for 12 hours

3 Tbs. maple syrup

1 cup water

1 tsp. vanilla extract

1 Tbs. cocoa powder

GOOD TO KNOW

Nut based ice creams and other frozen desserts are very popular in the vegan kitchen. But you don't have to be a vegan to enjoy these egg, flour and milk-free desserts. Even the cocoa powder can be substituted with vanilla extract and lemon.

長夏安中

ORANGE AND SWEET.
INTOXICATING SCENT
ON THE BREEZE AMIDST THE LEAVES
SH…SH…SH…
MOTHER EARTH
RESTING.

AVITAL SEBBAG

LATE SUMMER

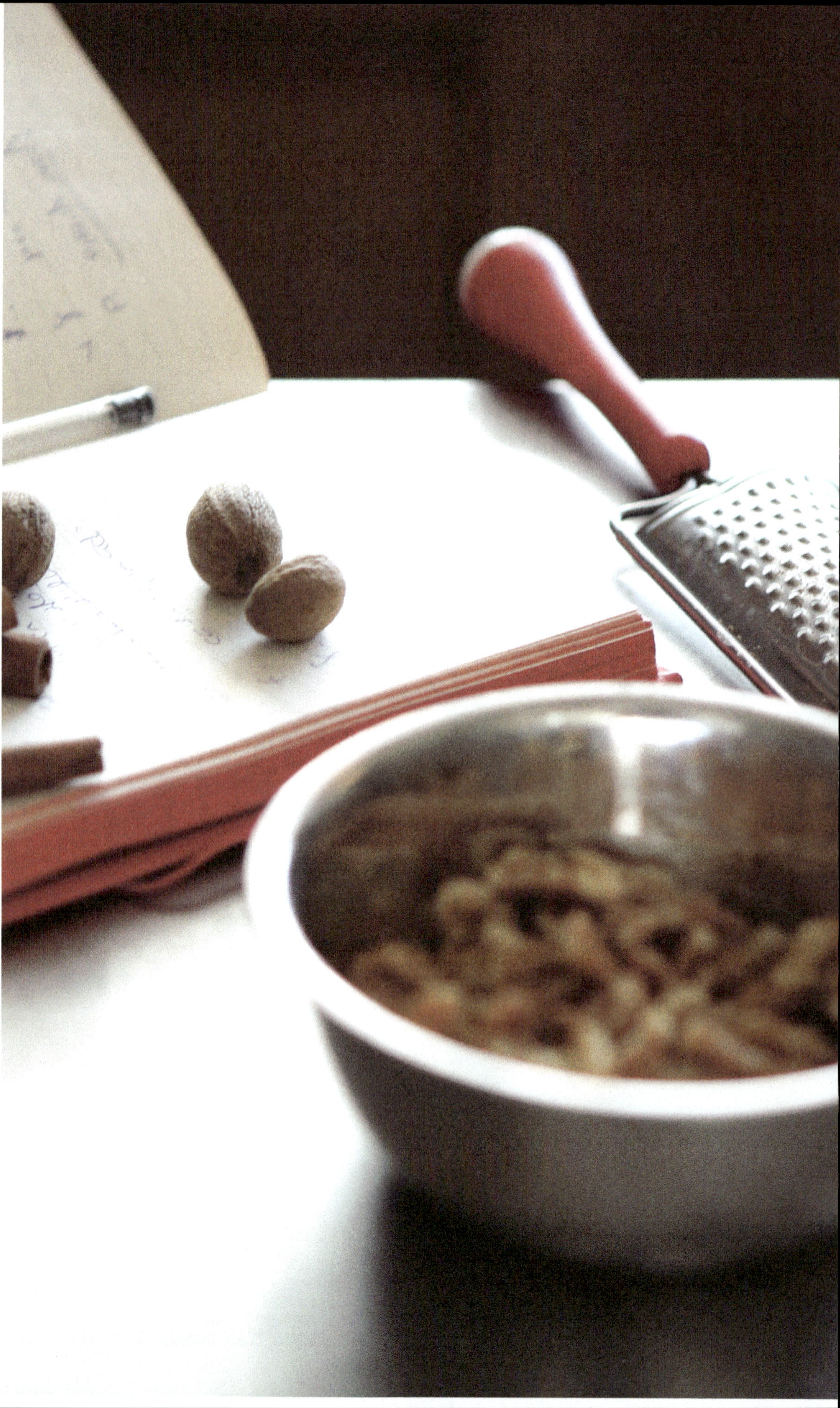

目錄

Late Summer

|94-95| Bright Orange Shake
|96-97| Tri-color Cashew Cheese Rolls
|98-99| Spreads
|100-101| Joy Crackers
|102| Puccini Zucchini
|103| Root Vegetables in Bamboo Steamer
|104-105| Zucchini Salad with Champignon Mushrooms and Radish
|106-107| Stuffed Round Squash
|108-109| Sweet Potato Gnocchi with Grilled Pepper and Kalamata Olive Sauce
|110-111| Chilled Orange Almond Cream Soup
|112-113| Milky Choco-Almond Shake
|114-115| Won-Kwang-Sa Pie
|116-119| Seasonal Fruit Ice Cream Cone
|120-121| Truffles
|122-123| Homemade Healing Chocolate

Bright Orange Shake

材料

Yields 2 liters

2 mangos,
peeled and pitted

4 figs

1 cup mint leaves

1 lime, peeled

4 walnuts

1 Tbs.
coconut oil

6 ice cubes

2 cups water

Blend all ingredients in a heavy duty blender until fully combined and smooth. Serve immediately.

95 | Late Summer

GOOD TO KNOW

To make hard cheese, substitute cashews with Macadamia nuts that have been dried in a food dehydrator at 41°C for 24 hours. The cheese will consolidate to a hard cheese texture.

長夏安中

Tri-color Cashew Cheese Rolls

Step 1

In a blender set at high speed, process ingredients into a fully incorporated mixture. Wrap in cheese cloth and place under a jar filled with water (this functions as a weight). Place in a colander set over a deep bowl and leave at room temperature for 24 hours until all the liquid is drained.

Step 2

Remove cheese from cloth, and process in a blender with lemon juice, salt and beer yeast. Divide cheese into 3 portions, placing each in a separate bowl. Add seasoning ingredients and mix. Place three 8 cm. aluminum rings on a flat plate. Transfer cheese mixtures to rings. Refrigerate for at least 12 hours.

Yields 3 rolls

Step 1

2 cups cashews, soaked for 2 hours

1 cup water

1 tsp. acidophilus probiotic powder (available in health food stores and drugstores)

Step 2

3/4 tsp. salt

2 tsp. beer yeast

1-2 tsp. lemon juice

Cheese Seasonings

Red

1/4 red bell pepper, chopped

4 sun dried tomatoes

1 tsp. dried oregano

1/4 red onion

1 tsp. paprika or 1/4 tsp. chili powder

Yellow

1/4 yellow bell pepper, chopped

1 tsp. turmeric

1 tsp. dried thyme

1 clove garlic

Green

1 clove garlic, crushed

1/2 tsp. ground black or white pepper

1/4 cup dill, chopped

2 scallions, finely chopped

Spreads

Sun-dried Tomatoes, Walnut and Ginger Spread

Yields 250 gr.

1 cup
sun-dried tomatoes

1 cup walnuts

1 tsp. coarse
Atlantic sea salt

1/2 tsp. coarsely
ground black pepper

2 cloves garlic

1 onion

1 Tbs. grated
fresh ginger root

juice from 1/2 a lemon

1/2 cup olive oil

1/2 cup water at
room temperature

Indian Pesto

Yields 250 gr.

1 bunch basil

1 bunch coriander

1/2 cup mint leaves

8 cloves garlic

1 cup olive oil

1 tsp. coarse
Atlantic sea salt

1-2 fresh or
dried chili pepper

1 tsp. lemon juice
(optional)

Sprouted Black Lentil and Walnut Spread

Yields 250 gr.

1 cup black lentils,
sprouted and cooked

5 sun-dried tomatoes

1/2 cup walnuts

1 cup parsley, chopped

2 Tbs. olive oil

1 tsp. cumin

1 tsp. coarse
Atlantic sea salt

juice from 1 lemon

Process all ingredients in a food processor to desired consistency.

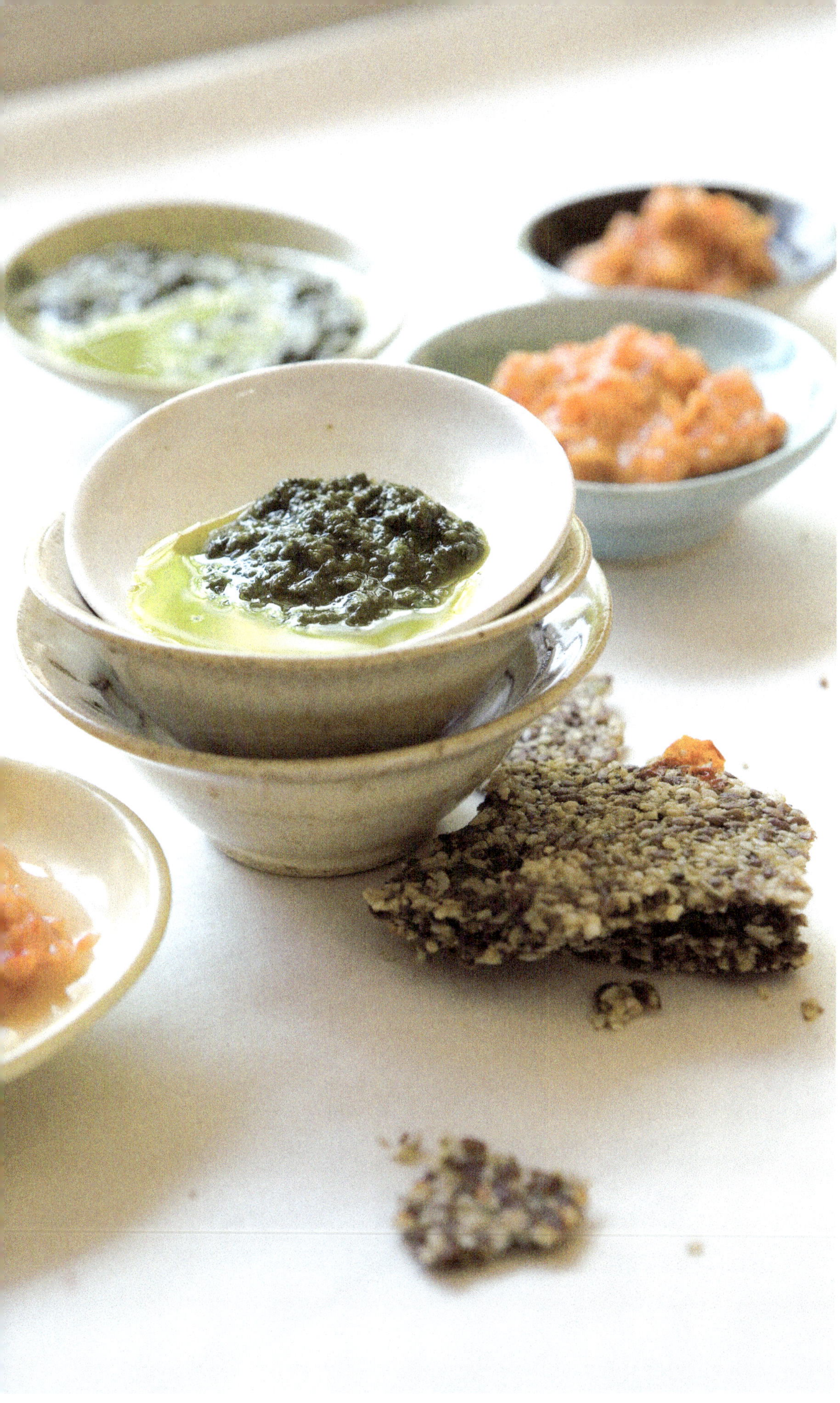

Joy Crackers

材料

Yields 500 gr.

100 gr. flax seeds

100 gr. sunflower seeds

100 gr. pumpkin seeds

100 gr. sesame seeds

100 gr. walnuts

1 fresh chili pepper

1/4 cup sun-dried tomatoes

1 tsp. coarse Atlantic sea salt

1 tsp. cumin

1 Tbs. olive oil

Soak all seeds for 2 hours. Squeeze out the liquid. In a food processor, combine seeds with the remaining ingredients and process for several minutes.

Thinly spread mixture on Teflex sheets. Dry in a food dehydrator at 40°C for 24 hours. If using a regular oven, preheat to 150°C. Line a baking pan with parchment paper. Using a spatula, thinly spread mixture onto paper. Bake for 30 minutes. Remove pan from oven, cut dough into squares using a sharp knife, return to oven and bake for 15 minutes. Turn crackers over and bake for an additional 15 minutes.

GOOD TO KNOW

These crispy, delicious crackers are an excellent addition to a gluten free diet or to help cleanse gluten from the body. Substitute spices with the seasoning of your choice. Flax seeds help cleanse the digestive system, and are particularly effective in relieving symptoms of Lazy Bowel Syndrome. When soaked for an hour or more, the seeds excrete a gummy substance that binds the ingredients together.

Puccini Zucchini

材料

Serves 8

6 zucchini

6 tomatoes

4 cloves garlic

1/4 cup
Kalamata olives

1 red onion

1/4 cup
sun-dried tomatoes

pinch chili pepper

1 cup fresh basil

3 sprigs fresh thyme

Using a vegetable peeler, slice zucchini into long thin strips (discard seeds). Process remaining ingredients in a food processor to a coarse consistency. Pour sauce over zucchini. Serve immediately.

GOOD TO KNOW

This is a fresh, chilled "raw food" dish. "Raw foods" retain the nutritional values of soluble fibers, vitamins and enzymes that are lost when heated to temperatures over 41°C. To serve this dish warm, I recommend heating the sauce over a low flame to desired temperature. This dish is an excellent substitute for wheat pasta. The zucchini can be replaced with carrots and cucumber or a combination of your choice.

102 | Five Seasons in the Kitchen

Root Vegetables in Bamboo Steamer

Serves 4
Bamboo Steamer

2 fennel

250 gr. pumpkin

2 sweet potatoes or carrots

2 small onions

2 kohlrabi

2 beets

1 round squash

To serve

1 Tbs. sesame seeds

1 tsp. coarse Atlantic sea salt

juice from 1/2 a lemon

1 tsp. ground black pepper

2 Tbs. tahini paste

Rinse vegetables and cut in half. Arrange in a bamboo steamer placed over a pot of boiling water. If a steamer is not available, use a vegetable or couscous steamer. Steam for 20 minutes or until vegetables are soft. Sprinkle with sesame seeds, pepper and coarse salt. Drizzle tahini and a few drops of lemon juice on top. Serve.

GOOD TO KNOW

Steamed vegetables are an easy, healthy snack or side dish that can be enjoyed year round by combining seasonal produce. Topped with tahini, this dish is a rich source of calcium and iron.

103 | Late Summer

Zucchini Salad with Champignon Mushrooms and Radish

Serves 4

2 zucchini

10 fresh Champignon mushrooms

2 celery stalks

5 basil leaves

1 radish

1/4 cup Hijiki, not soaked

Dressing

juice from 1/2 a lemon

1 tsp. mirin

1/2 tsp. black pepper

1/2 tsp. coarse Atlantic sea salt

1 Tbs. olive oil

Rinse vegetables thoroughly. Cut mushrooms, radish and zucchini into rounds and then in half. Chop celery stalks. Leave basil leaves whole. Place salad ingredients in a bowl. Mix dressing ingredients and pour over vegetables. Garnish with Hijiki.

GOOD TO KNOW

Hijiki is a salt water seaweed. It is rich in iron, iodine, calcium and anti-oxidants. For this salad, I use dried, flaky Hijiki. Hijiki can be soaked in water for 15 minutes, and added to a variety of cooked dishes and salads. Although changing after soaking, its taste is still delicious. I like both options.

STUFFED ROUND SQUASH

材料

Serves 4

4 round squash

10 Champignon mushrooms, chopped

1 cup Macadamia nuts

5 basil leaves

1 tsp. coarse Atlantic sea salt

1/2 tsp. chili oil

1 tsp. curry powder

2 Tbs. water or as needed

Preheat oven to 180°C. Slice off tops of squash, set aside. Using a teaspoon, scoop out and discard pulp. In a blender, process Macadamia nuts, basil and spices while adding water to reach desired consistency. Add to chopped mushrooms. Stuff squash with filling and cover with tops. Arrange squash on a baking pan lined with parchment paper or in an ovenproof dish. Bake for 30 minutes. Squash can also be baked in a food dehydrator at 41°C for 24 hours or more, as needed.

GOOD TO KNOW

Food enzymes are destroyed at temperatures over 41°C. Baking in a food dehydrator retains the enzymes nutritional values. I first became aware of the many benefits of using a food dehydrator through my interest in Raw Food nutrition (a dietary practice of eating uncooked, unprocessed foods only).

107 | Late Summer

Sweet Potato Gnocchi with
Grilled Pepper Sauce

Serves 4

2 sweet potatoes

1 cup
spelt flour

2 tsp. coarse
Atlantic sea salt

1/2 tsp. black pepper

5 basil leaves, chopped

chives for garnish

3 liters water

Sauce

3 bell peppers

2 cloves garlic

1/2 tsp. coarse
Atlantic sea salt

7 Kalamata olives, pitted

Peel sweet potatoes. Bake in preheated oven 200°C for 30 minutes or untill soft. Mash while still hot, gradually add flour, basil, 1 tsp. salt and 1/2 tsp. black pepper. Mix to dough-like texture. Set aside for 15 minutes. Divide dough into tennis ball size portions. Shape portions into long "snakes". Cut snakes into 1 cm. thick rounds.

In a deep pot, boil 3 liters water with 1 tsp. salt. Drop gnocchi into water and cook for 3-5 minutes after floating to the surface.

Sauce

Roast bell peppers over flame or in the oven until skin is charred. Place in a nylon bag for 15 minutes. Remove and peel. Transfer to a food processor or blender, add Kalamata olives, salt and 2 cloves garlic. Process until smooth.

To Serve

Ladle sauce onto plate, arrange gnocchi on top and garnish with chives.

GOOD TO KNOW

There are many varieties of sweet potato. In Chinese medicine, the sweet potato is associated with 'earth' due to its orange color and sweet taste. Its high fiber content helps maintain a healthy digestive system, and curbs cravings for sweets. This dish upgrades potato-based traditional gnocchi.

Late Summer

Chilled Orange Almond Cream Soup

材料

Serves 4

Almond Milk

1 cup almonds, soaked for 12 hours

1 cup water

Soup

4 celery stalks

1 finger (5-6 cm.) fresh ginger root

2 cloves garlic

1 tsp. fresh chili or chili oil

4 carrots

1 lemon

pinch black pepper

1/2 cup parsley leaves

Almond Milk

Process almonds and water in a blender. Transfer to cheese cloth. Wring over a bowl to extract almond milk.

Soup

In a juicer, juice carrots, celery, ginger and garlic to make a clear juice. Juice lemon using a hand juicer. Combine almond milk, vegetable juice, lemon juice and spices. Pour into soup bowls and garnish with parsley.

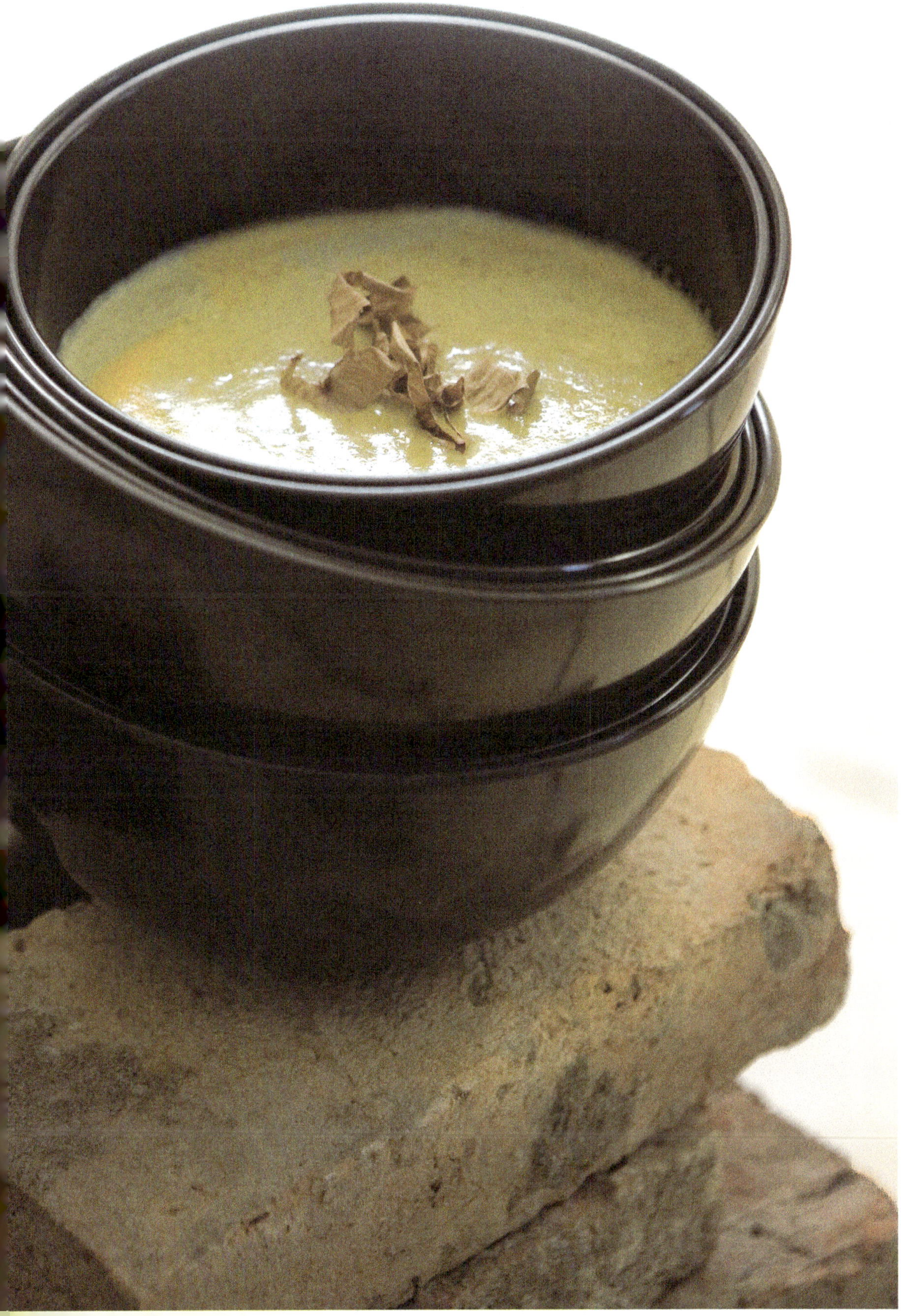

112 | Five Seasons in the Kitchen

Milky Choco-Almond Shake

Pour almond milk into a shaker or heavy duty blender. Add remaining ingredients and process to a smooth, fully incorporated consistency. Serve chilled.

材料

Yields 2 cups

1/2 liter
almond milk
(recipe on page 110)

2 Tbs. cocoa powder
(preferably from
unroasted beans)

2 tsp. maple syrup

1 tsp. cinnamon

4 dates, pitted

8 ice cubes

GOOD TO KNOW

The unroasted cocoa bean is the natural form of chocolate. Due to its unique mineral content and nutritional properties, natural cocoa is considered one of nature's super-foods. Rich in anti-oxidants, magnesium, iron and calcium, unroasted cocoa beans boost alertness and sexual arousal, and improve concentration, memory and blood flow.

Won-Kwang-Sa Pie

材料

For 26 cm. pie dish

Dough

2 cups walnuts

1 Tbs. coconut oil

4 dates, pitted

1 cup sugarless berry jam

Filling

3 Granny Smith apples

3 Tbs. coconut oil

4 Tbs. maple syrup

2 tsp. cinnamon

Chop walnuts in a food processor. Add 1 Tbs. coconut oil to make a smooth dough. Press the dough evenly onto the bottom of a pie dish. Spread jam over dough.

Peel and core apples. Cut into halves. In a pan, sweat apples in coconut oil for 4-5 minutes. Add maple syrup and cinnamon, and mix gently. Continue to cook until liquids are absorbed. Arrange apples in a swirl pattern on top of the dough. Cover and refrigerate for 1 hour.

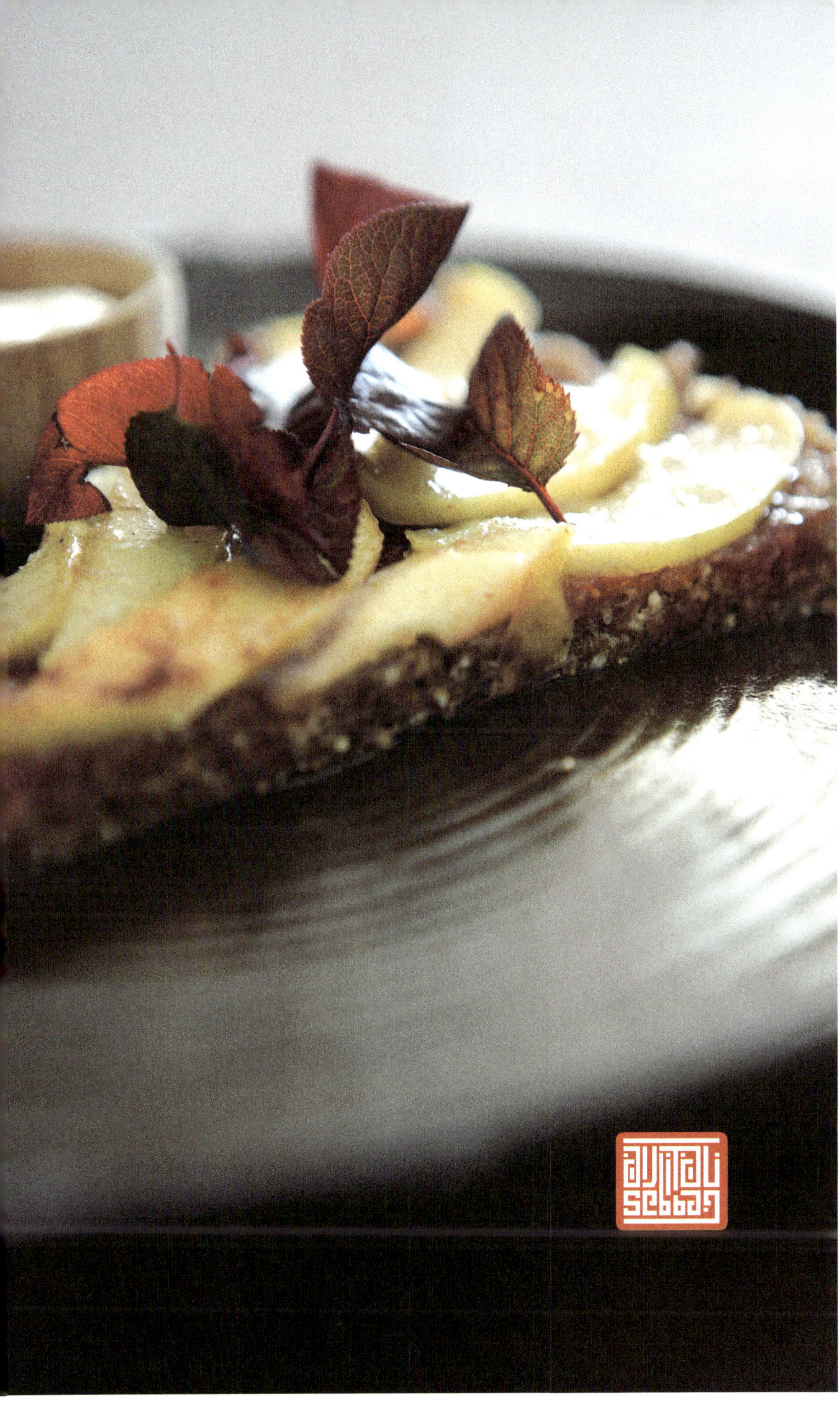

Seasonal Fruit Ice Cream Cone

Yields 8 cones

Cone

1 cup flax seed, ground into flour

1/2 cup cashews, ground into flour

1/2 cup spelt, finely ground into flour

3 Tbs. lemon juice

3 Tbs. date honey or maple syrup

1/2 tsp. coarse Atlantic sea salt

2 tsp. vanilla extract

1 pear, peeled and cored

1/2 cup water

1/2 cup almonds, coarsely ground

1/4 cup pistachios, coarsely ground

Cone

In food processor, process flours with all ingredients except almonds and pistachios. Transfer to a bowl, add almonds and pistachios, and combine into an elastic dough. Roll the dough into a 12 cm. diameter round and place on an oven grid lined with parchment paper or Teflex. Dry in the oven at 150°C for 15 minutes, or in a food dehydrator at 41°C for 4-5 hours.

Cut dough into rounds using a 12 cm. diameter ring. Roll into cones, securing bottoms with toothpicks. Oven dry on unlined oven grid for 15 minutes, or in a food hydrator for 4 hours until cones are crispy.

Late Summer

SEASONAL FRUIT ICE CREAM CONE

Ice cream

Yields 1 kg.

500 gr. seasonal fruit. (in late summer, I recommend using mango, melon, black plums or fresh figs).

1 cup coconut oil

500 gr. cashews, soaked for 12 hours

1 cup pistachios

1 cup almonds, soaked for 12 hours

1 cup mint leaves, rinsed

2 cups ice cubes

zest from 1 lemon

1 Tbs. ground ginger root

Blend all ingredients to a coarse consistency. Freeze for 2 hours. Fill cones with ice cream and serve.

I recommend using a heavy-duty blender.

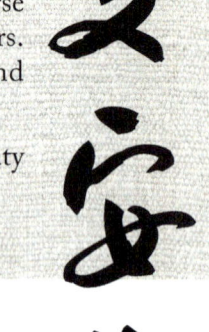

GOOD TO KNOW

Making ice cream with your kids guarantees hours of quality time and fun with the extra benefit of teaching them how delicious ice cream can be without using milk, food coloring, artificial preservatives and gluten.

119 | Late Summer

Truffles

材料

Yields 20

3/4 cup
almond butter

1/2 cup maple syrup
or rice malt

1/2 tsp. vanilla extract

1/3 cup cocoa powder

1/3 cup cocoa butter,
melted

pinch coarse
Atlantic sea salt

1/4 cup water

Optional toppings

finely ground coconut

ground pistachio nuts

cinnamon-cocoa
powder combination

In a blender, process all truffle ingredients to a fully incorporated and thick consistency. Refrigerate for at least 12 hours or until cream is hardened. Using an ice cream scoop, create large balls. Cut in half and form small identically sized balls. Gently roll in the coating of your choice. Keep refrigerated.

GOOD TO KNOW

This recipe is based on a recipe from the Matthew Kenny Academy of Oklahoma City. Promoting raw-super-vegan cuisine, the academy's restaurant is testimony to Kenny's conviction that vegans can savor the wonderful flavors nature has to offer.

Homemade Healing Chocolate

材料

1 1/2 cups cocoa powder

1 1/2 cups coconut oil

1 cup maple syrup, rice malt or date honey

Optional Additions (1 cup each)

ground almonds

coarsely ground pistachio nuts

Goji berries (available dried at health food stores)

cranberries

grated orange zest

grated lemon zest

cocoa shavings

coconut shavings

Mix dry and wet ingredients until fully incorporated. If coconut oil is consolidated, melt in a bain marie. Add additions of your choice.

Pour mixture into praline molds.

Note: Additions should be prepared in quantities of 1 cup each. If using more than one, combine to produce 1 cup. For instance: 1/4 cup ground pistachios, 1/4 cup cranberries and 1/2 cup cocoa shavings.

BE SILENT
SCATTERED AUTUMN SHOWERS
GOING OUT TO GATHER FOOD
TO COLLECT
SPRING WATER

ZEN MASTER RYOKAN

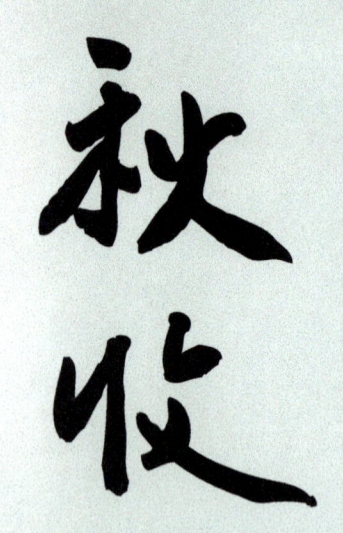

AUTUMN

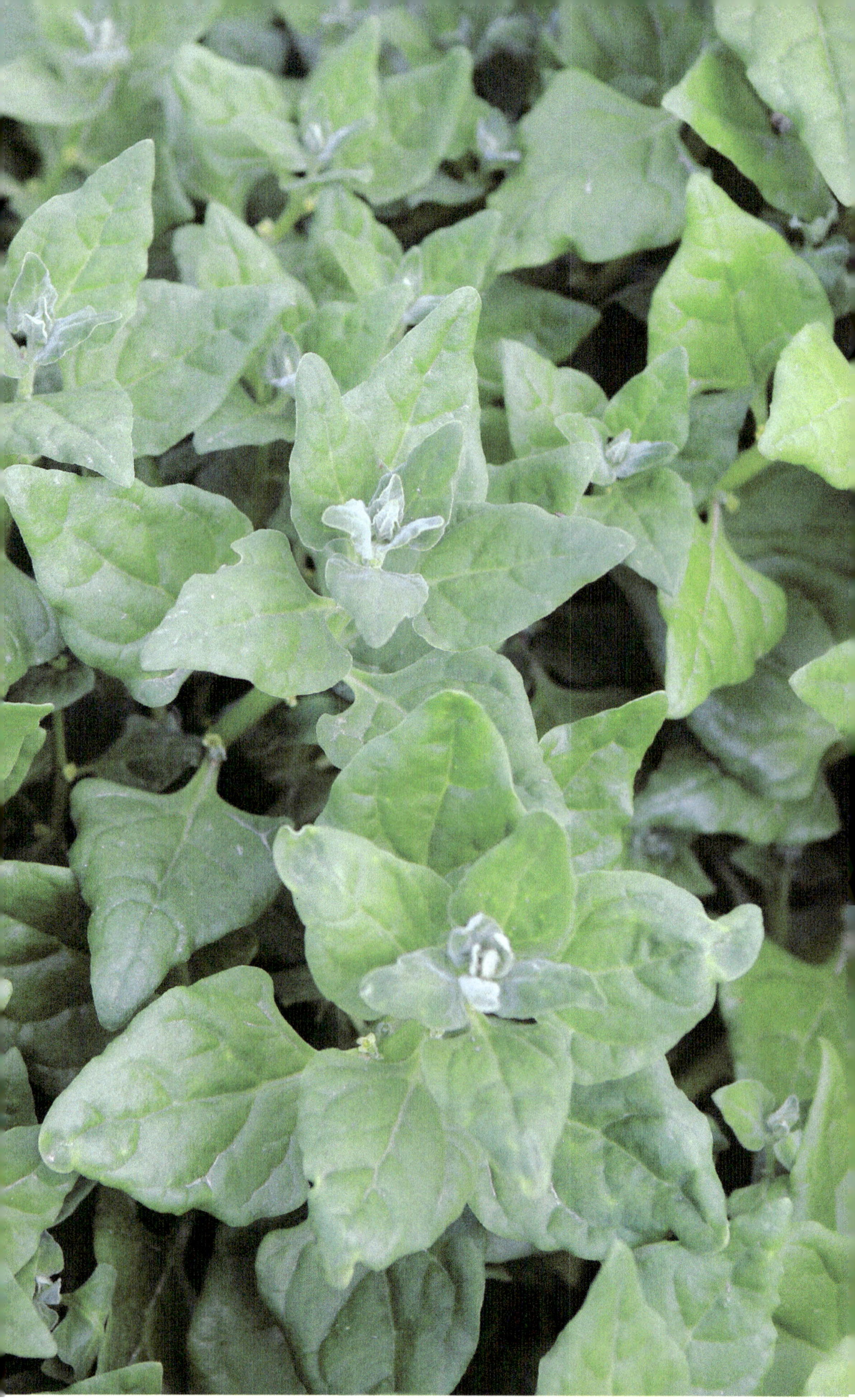

目錄

Autumn

| |128-129| Vegetable and Tofu Antipasti
| |130-131| King Oyster St. Jacques in Lemon Sauce
| |132-133| Creamy Lentil Soup
| |134-135| Traditional Couscous
| |136-137| Colorful Paella with Fresh Shitake Mushrooms
| |138-139| Stir Fried Tofu with Seasonal Green Beans
| |142-143| Hearty Root Soup
| |144-145| Three Variations on Tofu Kebabs
| |146| Pomacello Aperitif
| |147| Açai Sorbet
| |148| Eggplant and Zucchini Rolls
| |149| Cauliflower and Pumpkin in Macadamia Cream
| |150-151| Bite-size Beet and Zucchini Rolls

Vegetable and Tofu Antipasti

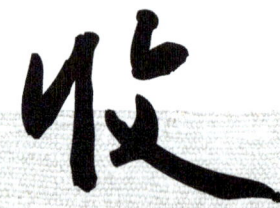

Serves 4

1 eggplant

1 red bell pepper

500 gr. Jerusalem artichokes

1 sweet potato

1 kohlrabi

1 beet

1 turnip

2 heads garlic

100 gr. tofu

1 Tbs. soy sauce

Sauce

3 cloves garlic, crushed

1/4 cup olive oil

1 tsp. herb salt

Preheat oven to 180°C. Dice the tofu and marinate for 15 minutes in 2 Tbs. water and 1 Tbs. soy sauce. Rinse vegetables thoroughly and cut into 1 cm. thick slices. Rinse garlic heads and leave whole. Arrange vegetables and tofu on a baking pan lined with parchment paper. Mix all sauce ingredients in a separate bowl. Using a brush, coat vegetables generously with sauce and roast for 15 minutes. Turn vegetables over and roast for an additional 15 minutes.

GOOD TO KNOW

Herb salt adds that extra pizzazz to a wide variety of dishes. It's easy to make – here's how: sun dry an assortment of fresh herbs such as thyme, oregano and rosemary. When dry, crush herbs using a mortar and pestle (your fingers will also do). Combine 1/2 cup of herbs with 1 cup coarse Atlantic sea salt. Bon appetite!

129 | Autumn

KING OYSTER ST. JACQUES IN LEMON SAUCE

Serves 4

4 King Oyster mushrooms

1 tsp. sesame seeds

Marinade

1 Tbs. ginger root, grated

3 garlic cloves

1 Tbs. sesame oil

juice from 2 lemons

1 Tbs. soy sauce

Garnish

1 tsp. Hijiki

Slice mushrooms into 1/2 cm. rounds. Mix marinade ingredients and marinate mushrooms for 1 hour. Drain and arrange mushrooms on food dehydrator pan (save marinade). Dry at 41°C for 6 hours. Alternatively, arrange mushrooms on a cookie sheet and bake in the oven at 150°C for 30 minutes.

To serve: drizzle 1 tsp. marinade over mushrooms, sprinkle with sesame seeds and garnish with a strand of Hijiki.

GOOD TO KNOW

This is a vegetarian version of scallops in a creamy butter and wine sauce. Originating in China, the King Oyster mushroom is rich in anti-oxidants. Known for its unique flavor and meaty texture, this low calorie mushroom is a perfect sea-food substitute.

131 | Autumn

Creamy Black Lentil Soup

GOOD TO KNOW

Lentils are a popular staple in India where they are served with Basmati rice.

Soak lentils for 8 hours. Drain and sprout for 1 day, rinsing at least twice. Grate tomato, garlic and ginger. Combine with spices in a small bowl, transfer to a medium size pot and sweat lightly in olive oil. Add lentils and water. Bring to the boil. Lower heat and simmer for 2 hours or until lentils are soft. If you like your soup extra smooth, blend with a hand blender.

Serves 8

500 gr. small (beluga) black lentils

6 garlic cloves

1 tomato

1 finger (6 cm.) ginger root

1 tsp. ground cumin

1 tsp. black pepper

2 tsp. curry powder

1 tsp. course Atlantic sea salt

1 Tbs. olive oil

4 liters water (to cover ingredients)

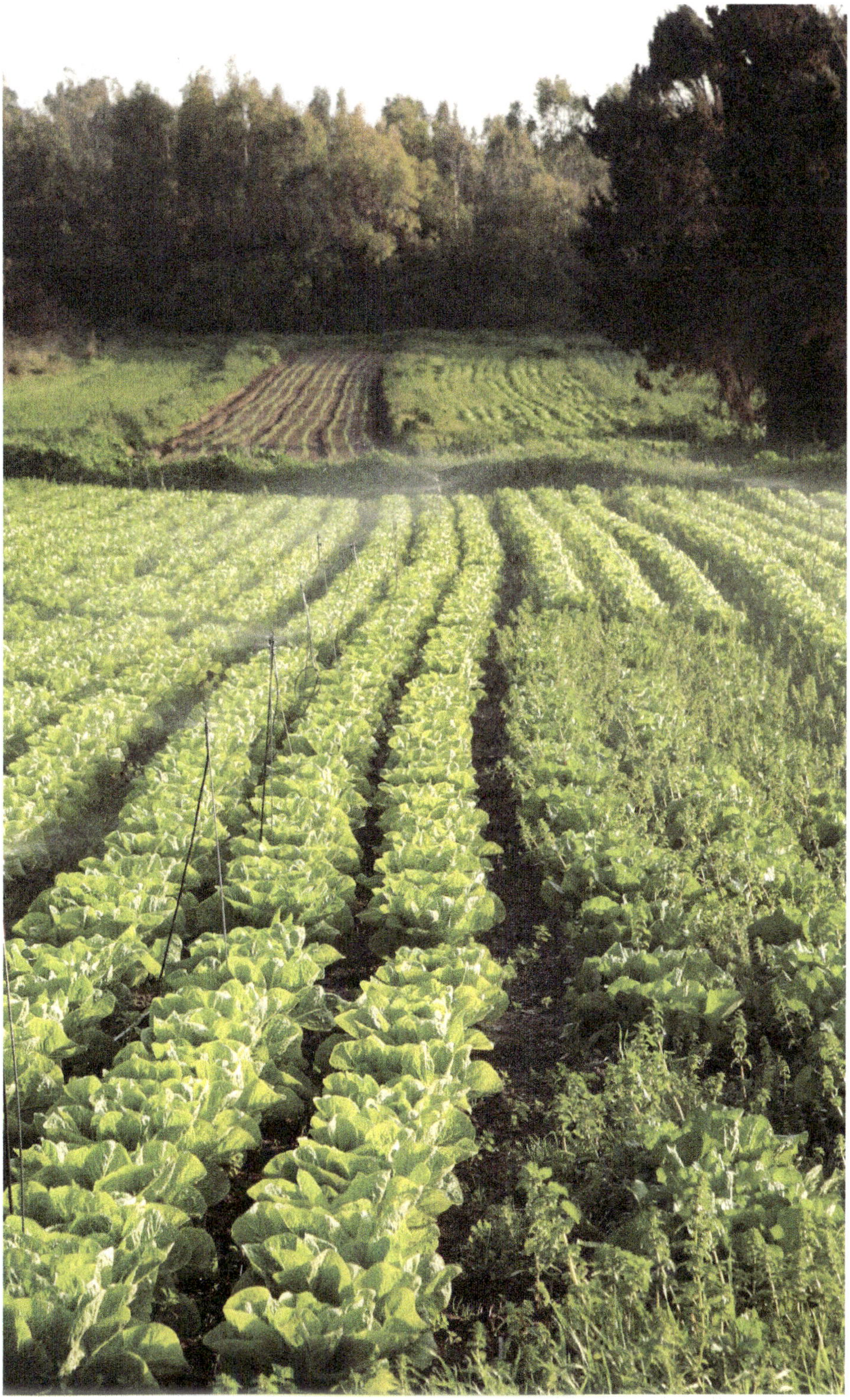

Traditional Moroccan Couscous

材料

Serves 6

Soup

100 gr. dried chickpeas

250 gr. pumpkin

1 zucchini

3 carrots

1 parsley root

1 celery root

5 celery stalks

1/2 cauliflower

1/4 green cabbage

1 turnip

1 leek

2 garlic cloves

1 onion

1/2 cup coriander leaves, chopped

1/2 cup parsley leaves, chopped

2 tsp. Baharat (Middle Eastern spice mix)

2 tsp. turmeric

1 tsp. ground black pepper

2 Tbs. course Atlantic sea salt

8 cups water

Soup

Place chickpeas in a large bowl and cover with cold tap water. Soak for a minimum of 8 hours. Make sure to change the water twice. Rinse and sprout for 24 hours. Place chickpeas in a pressure cooker or large pot. Cook for 1 1/2 hours or until chickpeas are soft but not mushy. Rinse the vegetables, cut into large pieces and place in the bottom of a couscous pot. Add just enough water to cover the vegetables. Add spices and chickpeas and bring to the boil. Lower heat and simmer for 1 hour and 20 minutes. In the meantime, soak coriander and parsley in water for 15 minutes. Add to soup and cook for an additional 10 minutes. For kids who might prefer soup without leaves, tie parsley and coriander with string, place in soup and remove before serving.

Traditional Steamed Couscous

Combine all couscous ingredients in a bowl, cover with water and let stand for 5 minutes. Transfer to top part (colander) of couscous pot. Gently rub couscous between the palms of your hands to separate lumps. Steam over soup on low heat for 20 minutes. If not serving immediately, remove colander and cover with a small towel.

Traditional Service: place 4 Tbs. couscous in a soup bowl. Add 3-4 Tbs. vegetables and chickpeas (without liquid). Add approximately 1/2 cup soup to lightly saturate couscous.

Couscous

1 package whole grain couscous (100 gr.)

1 Tbs. olive oil

1 tsp. salt

2 cups boiling water

1/4 tsp. turmeric

GOOD TO KNOW

Traditional Moroccan couscous is made with white, ground and processed semolina. In my mother's house, couscous meals marked the coming of autumn and the beginning of the Jewish New Year. Some of the ingredients in this recipe are substituted with healthier options; the processed semolina is replaced with more nutritious whole grain semolina. Semolina bran contains soluble fibers that cleanse the digestive system; its sprouts contain vitamin E that protect the skin against the hazards free radicals.

135 | Autumn

Colorful Paella with Fresh Shitake Mushrooms

Preheat oven to 180°C. Dice tofu and mushrooms, and marinate in soy sauce, ginger and curry for 1 hour. Soak rice in tap water for 30 minutes, drain and leave to dry in colander. Roast saffron threads in the paella pot for 3 minutes. Remove and set aside in a small bowl. Add leeks and garlic to pot and sauté in olive oil until lightly browned. Add rice, vegetables, spices and saffron threads. Mix and add broth or water. Bring to the boil, lower the heat and simmer for 7 minutes. Place in oven and bake for 20 minutes. Add tofu and mushrooms and bake for an additional 10 minutes.

Garnish with chopped cilantro and serve.

Serves 4

Large Dutch Oven or
oven-proof pot with fitted lid

500 gr. whole
Basmati rice

2 leeks,
sliced into rounds

2 celery stalks,
chopped

1/2 package Hijiki,
soaked in water

4 garlic cloves,
chopped

1 red bell pepper,
diced into small cubes

1 large tomato,
peeled and diced

100 gr. tofu

10 fresh
Shitake mushrooms

4 King Oyster
mushrooms

2 tsp. olive oil

1 Tbs. course
Atlantic sea salt

2 Tbs. soy sauce

1/2 tsp. curry powder

2 Tbs. grated ginger root

1/2 tsp. chili powder

1 tsp. ground
black pepper

20 saffron threads,
soaked in 1/4 cup
hot water

3 cups vegetable
broth or water

1 cup chopped cilantro

GOOD TO KNOW

This recipe is quick, healthy and wholesome 'fast food'. Substitute ingredients with whatever's in season or with whatever's available in your fridge. Delicious both hot and cold.

STIR FRIED татоFU WITH
SEASONAL GREEN BEANS

Serves 4

1 package (200 gr.) tofu, cubed

1/2 cup Hijiki

1 1/2 onions, sliced into strips

500 gr. fresh green beans, trimmed and halved

4 Shitake mushrooms, quartered

2 King Oyster mushrooms, quartered

1 Portobello mushroom, quartered

1 tsp. fresh grated ginger root

1 tsp. curry powder

1/2 tsp. course Atlantic sea salt

1/4 cup black or white sesame seeds

2 Tbs. olive or sesame oil

2 cloves garlic, grated

2 Tbs. soy sauce

Soak Hijiki in cold water for 15 minutes, rinse and drain. In a heated wok, stir fry tofu, 1 Tbs. oil, salt and curry until tofu is golden. Set aside. Sauté onions in 1 Tbs. oil until golden. Add garlic and sauté for 2-3 minutes. Add green beans and stir fry for a few minutes longer. Add mushrooms and stir fry for 3-4 minutes. Add tofu and Hijiki, mix and sprinkle with sesame seeds.

While working on this book, I lost several dear friends and family members who accompanied me on my journey and played significant roles in my life.

One of them was my father, Gaby Sebbag, whose passing made me realize how blessed I was to have matured by his side, and the true meaning of loss.

An ending and a beginning, a beginning and an end, and so forth.

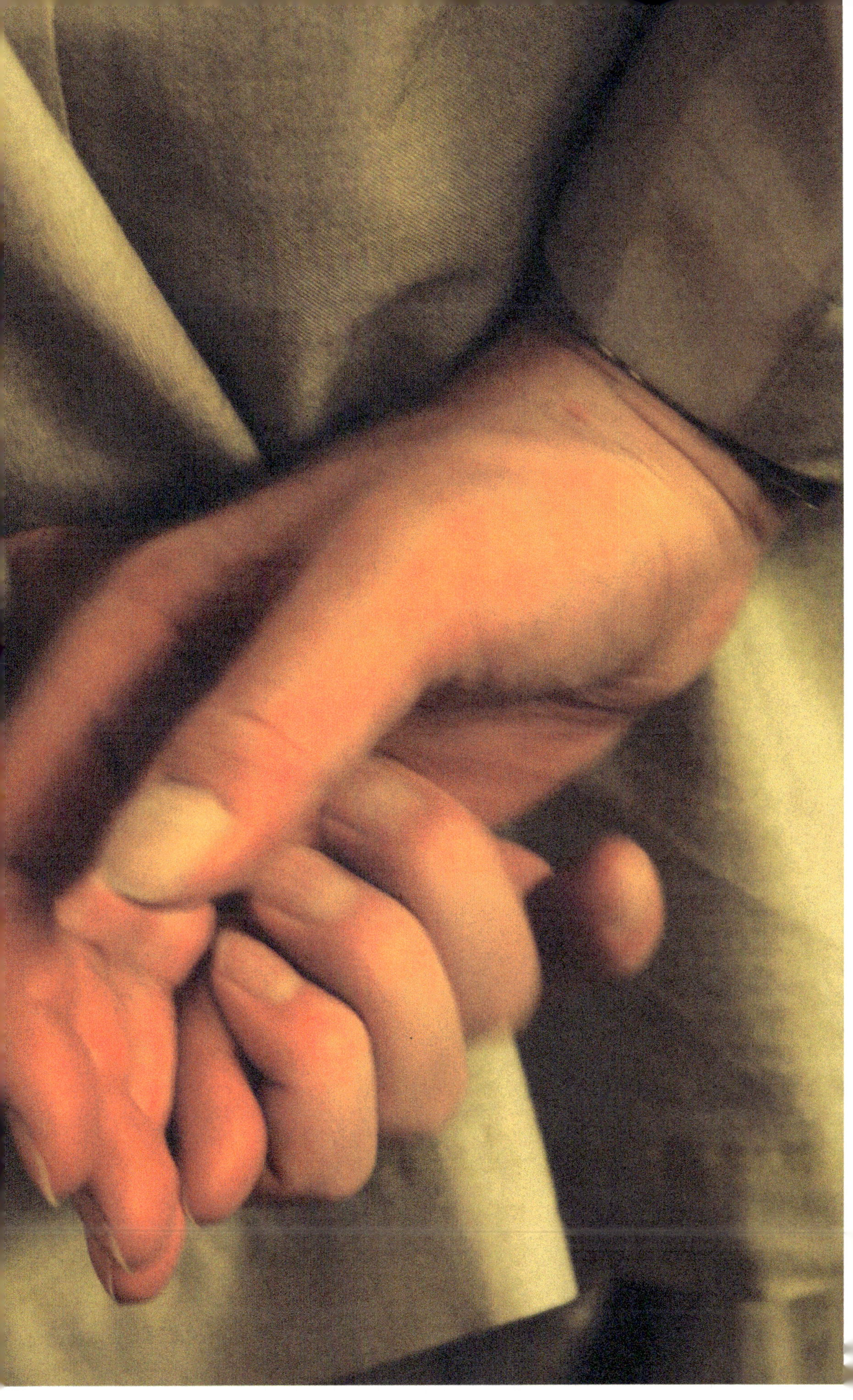

Hearty Root Soup

Serves 6

1 large onion

1 parsley root

10 Champignon mushrooms

2 fennel

2 cups cauliflower, cut into florets

1 celery root, including stalks

3 cloves garlic

2 cups chopped coriander

2 cups chopped parsley

1 tsp. coarse Atlantic sea salt

1 tsp. caraway seeds

1 Tbs. grated ginger root

1 whole chili pepper

3 liters water

Rinse all thoroughly, and cut into large cubes. Place vegetables in a large pot, add spices and water to cover. Bring to the boil, lower heat and simmer for 1 1/2 hours. Puree in a blender or in the pot using a hand blender. Divide into soup bowls, drizzle with 2 drops olive oil and a drop of lemon juice.

GOOD TO KNOW

Hot spices help strengthen the lungs. Using them in autumn boosts the immune system and prepares the body for winter – a natural immunization shot!

143 | Autumn

Three Variations on Tofu Kebabs

Yields 6 skewers

300 gr. tofu

1 red bell pepper

6 shallots, halved

1 zucchini

Cut tofu into 2 cm. cubes (approx. 24 cubes), and divide into three equal portions. In three separate bowls, combine ingredients for each marinade. Marinate tofu portions for 1 hour. Cut zucchini into 2 cm. thick rounds. Cut red pepper into equally sized squares. Push skewers through tofu cubes and vegetables. Grill on BBQ or grill pan. Turn until lightly browned on all sides.

Mediterranean marinade

1 tsp. paprika (sweet or hot)

1 tsp. cumin

1 clove garlic

2 Tbs. olive oil

Japanese marinade

2 Tbs. soy sauce

1 tsp. rice malt

1 Tbs. sesame oil

1 clove garlic

Indian marinade

1 tsp. curry powder

1 tsp. tandoori paste

1 tsp. chili oil

2 Tbs. olive oil

1/2 tsp. coarse Atlantic sea salt

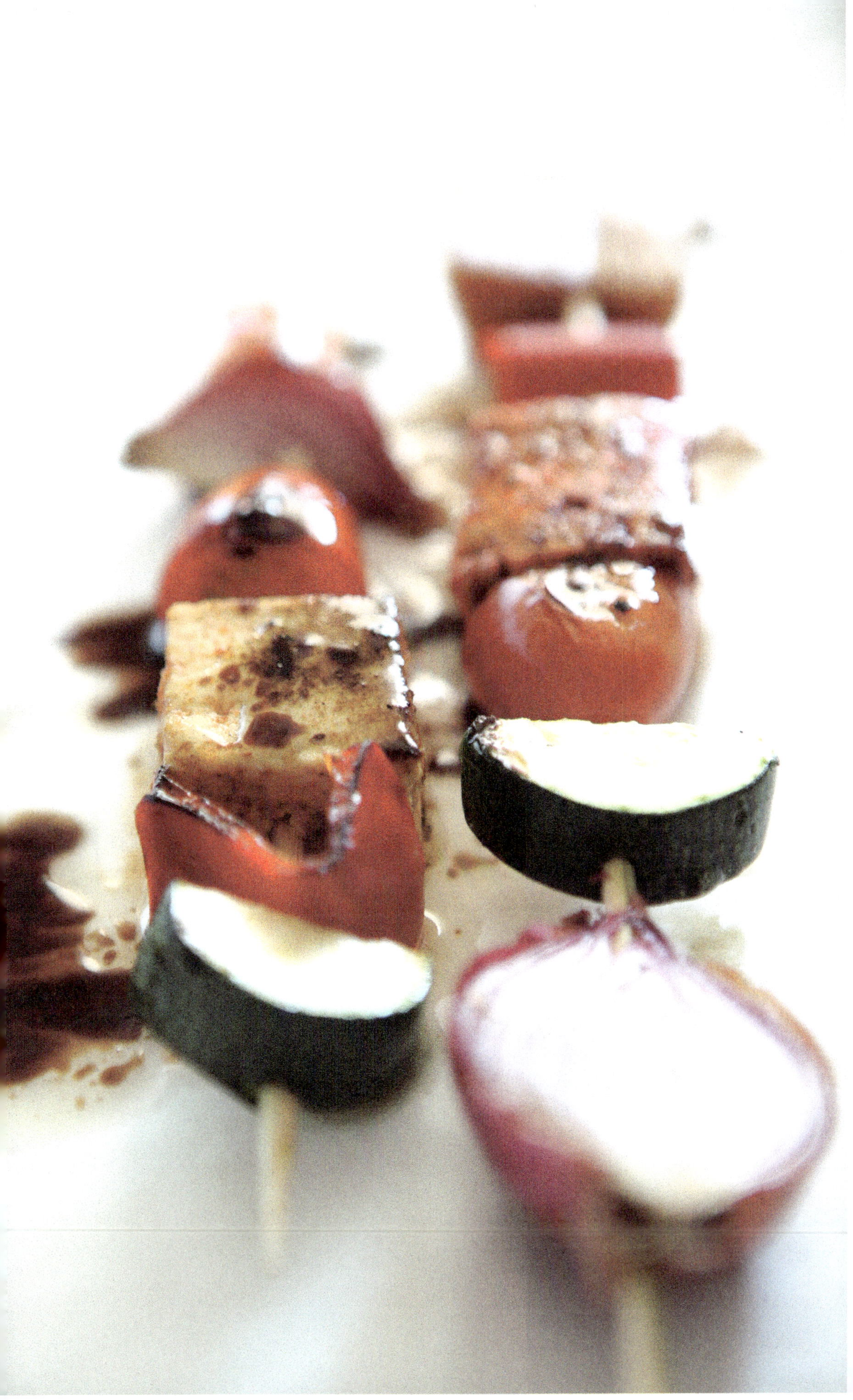

Pomacello Aperitif

Serves 4

4 pomegranates

16 ice cubes

1 Tbs. date honey, maple syrup or molasses

1 tsp. grated ginger root

juice from 1 lemon

GOOD TO KNOW

In Jewish tradition the pomegranate symbolizes blessings, wealth, beauty and wisdom. Its many properties include anti-oxidants, iron and a variety of vitamins and minerals that help decrease blood pressure and cholesterol as well as inhibiting various types of cancer. Pomegranate seeds are a great addition to salads; its juice makes a healthy, thirst-quenching drink.

In a blender, crush ice with date honey, ginger and lemon juice. Juice pomegranates using an electric or hand press juicer. Combine pomegranate juice with ice mixture. Pour into glasses and garnish with pomegranate seeds.

146 | Five Seasons in the Kitchen

Açai Sorbet

GOOD TO KNOW

Açai is cultivated in Brazil. It is considered a super anti-oxidant, and a rare source of Vitamin E. Açai is rich in iron, fatty acids and calcium.

Yields 2-3 cups

200 gr. frozen Açai

2 ripe mangos

3 Tbs. date honey

1 banana

10 ice cubes

1 lime, peeled

Combine all ingredients in a blender. Blend until smooth. Serve immediately.

147 | Autumn

Eggplant and Zucchini Rolls

Cut zucchini and eggplant into thin slices. Arrange on a roasting pan and roast in the oven, or sear on a lightly oiled heavy pan over a high flame. Cool. Place 1 tsp. Macadamia nut cheese in the center of each slice and top with a basil leaf. Roll.

Yields 22 rolls

1 zucchini

1 eggplant

22 basil leaves, rinsed

1/2 cup Macadamia nut cheese (recipe on page 170)

CAULIFLOWER AND PUMPKIN IN
MACADAMIA NUT CHEESE

Preheat oven to 180°C. Rinse cauliflower and pumpkin thoroughly. Soak cauliflower in salted water for 15 minutes. Divide into florets. Cut pumpkin into 1/2 cm. wedges and arrange on a baking pan lined with parchment paper. Process cream ingredients with 1/2 cup water in a heavy duty blender. Gradually add water until you've reached the desired consistency. Using a spatula, spread cream on cauliflower and pumpkin. Bake for 45 minutes.

Serves 4

1 cauliflower

250 gr. pumpkin

1 Tbs. coarse Atlantic sea salt

Cream

1 cup Macadamia nuts, soaked for 12 hours

1 cup cashews, soaked for 12 hours

1/2 cup water

1 shallot

2 cloves garlic

1 Tbs. white miso

1/2 tsp. turmeric

juice from 1/2 a lemon

BITE-SIZE BEET AND ZUCCHINI ROLLS

Yields 10

1 beet

1 zucchini

1 carrot

1 cucumber

4 scallions

10 chives

1 cup sunflower sprouts

1 cup mung bean sprouts

Pesto sauce for zucchini
(recipe on page 98)

Asian dressing for beets
(recipe on page 73)

To save time, I recommend using a mandolin slicer for this recipe.

Rinse vegetables and pat dry. Slice beets into 1 mm. thick wedges. Slice zucchini into 3 mm. thick rounds. Julienne carrot, cucumber and scallions. Place 1 tsp. pesto on the top edge of each zucchini slice. Stack 3 carrot juliennes, 3 cucumber juliennes, a small bunch each of sunflower and mash bean sprouts and a slice of scallion. Roll and tie with 2 chives. Repeat with beets and Asian sauce.

150 | Five Seasons in the Kitchen

GOOD TO KNOW

This dish is the star of cocktail catering, and a perfect "raw food" appetizer. Its fresh and colorful ingredients provide a unique opportunity to savor the wholesome flavors of vegetables that are usually not consumed raw, such as beets and zucchini.

冬藏

HOT STEW
AND THE SCENT OF SPICES
FILL
THE HOUSE
WARM
AND OUTSIDE IT IS COLD.
AVITAL SEBBAG

WINTER

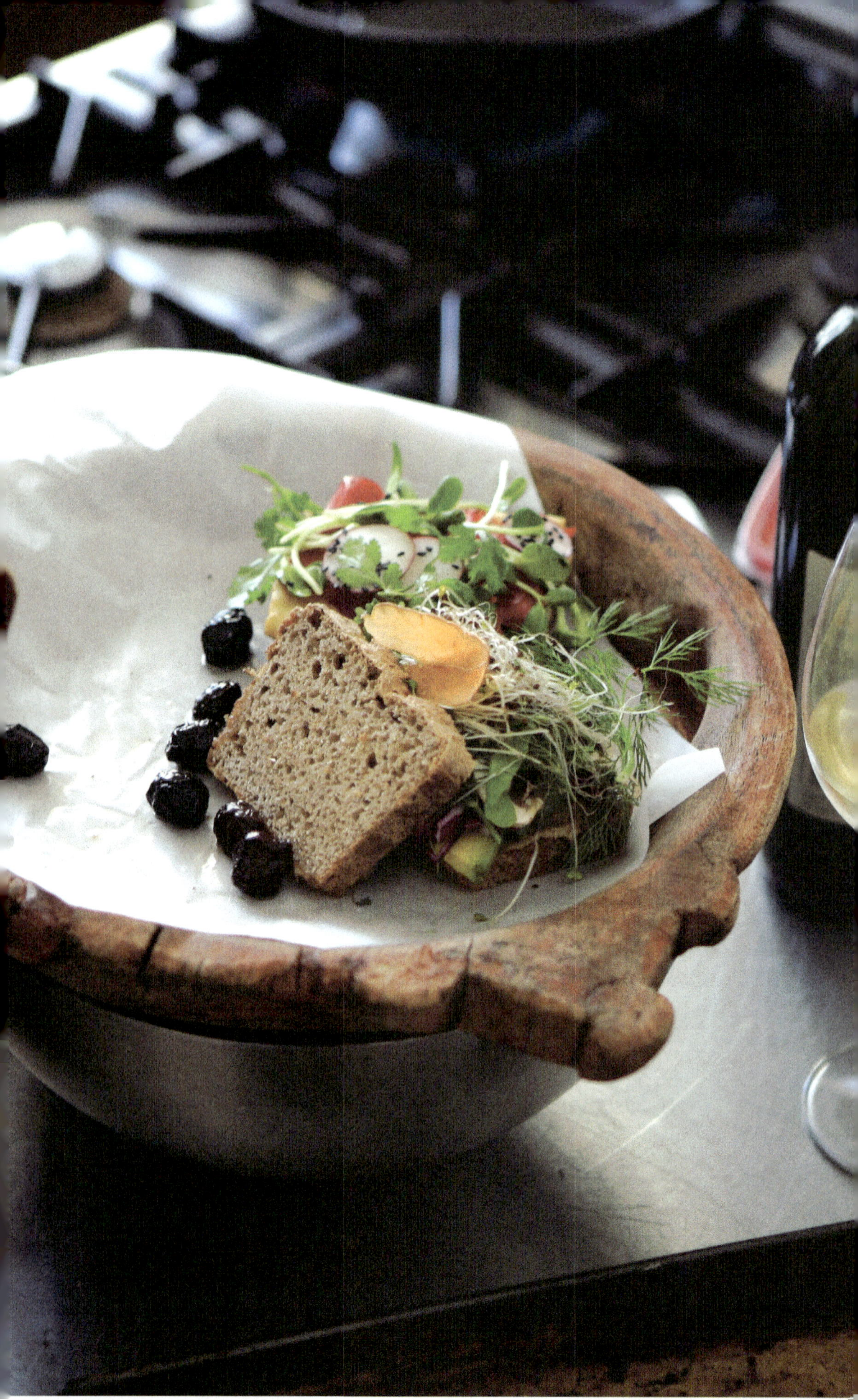

目錄

Winter

	156-157		Sunny Winter Drink
	158-159		Yellow Lentil Soup with a Twist
	160-161		Korean Miso Soup
	162-163		Healthy Winter Sandwich
	164-165		Tricolor Seaweed and Vegetable Winter Salad
	166-167		Stir-fried Mushrooms, Bok choy and Endive on a Bed of Bulgur
	168-169		Gimbap – Korean Sushi
	170-171		Stuffed Mushrooms with Macadamia Nut Cheese
	172-173		Mom's Homemade Chickpea Bean Stew
	174-175		Spelt Rolls
	176-177		Root Vegetable and Tofu Stew
	178-179		Moroccan Style Jerusalem Artichokes
	180-181		Pickled Vegetables – Kimchi in a Pickling Kettle
	182-183		Stir-fried Tempeh with Jerusalem Artichokes
	184-185		Bean, Lentil and Mushroom "Mesabaha"
	186-187		Rolled Oats Porridge
	188		Spice Cake
	189		Strawberry Sorbet

GOOD TO KNOW

Limes and lemons have extraordinary antiseptic qualities. That's why I keep them in my kitchen all year round. Although sour, lemons and limes are a basic staple, recommended as wonderful accompaniments to watermelon, grapefruit and mango. The color and subtle flavors of citrus fruit and honey remind me of that are usually not consumed raw, such as beets and zucchini: rays of winter's sun.

Sunny Winter Drink

Peel oranges and lime, and cut into large cubes. Rinse apples and ginger (do not peel). Place all ingredients in a heavy duty blender. Add water and blend until smooth and fully combined.

材料

Yields 2 liters

4 oranges

4 limes

4 Granny Smith apples

2-3 cm. ginger root

1 Tbs. coconut oil

2 Tbs. date honey

1/2 cup water

Yellow Lentil Soup with a Twist

Serves 8

500 gr. yellow lentils

1 onion

2 leeks

2 yellow bell peppers

1 medium cauliflower

2 fennel

1 Tbs. olive oil

1 tsp. turmeric

1 tsp. caraway seeds

1 fresh red chili pepper or 1 tsp. chili oil

pinch "4 seasons" pepper

1 Tbs. coarse Atlantic sea salt

5 liters water

Garnish

1 package mung bean sprouts

juice from 1 lemon

1 Tbs. ground hyssop

Soak lentils overnight. Rinse until water runs clear. Rinse all vegetables thoroughly and dice. Stir-fry vegetables in a soup pot with olive oil for a few minutes. Add spices and stir-fry for 2-3 minutes. Add lentils and water. Bring to the boil. Reduce heat and cook for 30 minutes. Using a hand blender or food processor, blend until smooth and fully combined. Garnish with sprouts, hyssop and a drop of lemon juice.

GOOD TO KNOW

This cauliflower, fennel and lentil combination is surprisingly unique. The soup's yellow color compliments its hearty, warm flavors. The spicy chili pepper enhances the blood flow and warms the body on cold winter days.

Korean Miso Soup

Serves 10

2 parsley roots

2 celery roots

6 celery stalks, chopped

6 carrots

2 onions

6 liters water

1/2 cup Wakame or Kombu seaweed

8 Shitake mushrooms

5 cloves garlic

1 package (250 gr.) mung bean sprouts

1 cup dark brown, organic miso

200 gr. tofu, cubed

Rinse all vegetables thoroughly. Soak seaweed and Shitake mushrooms in lukewarm water for 15 minutes. Rinse thoroughly. Quarter onions and slice carrots into thin rounds. Cut celery and parsley roots into 2 cm. slices. Place vegetables and water in a large pot, bring to the boil, reduce heat and cook for 30 minutes.

Before serving: mix miso with 1 cup cold water and add to pot. Place 1/4 cup tofu cubes and sprouts in soup bowls, add soup and serve.

GOOD TO KNOW

Miso ("Chiang" in Chinese) is made from soy beans and is prepared in most Korean households. Its origin is most probably in China where it was a staple in vegetarian Buddhist cuisine. Prepared through a fermentation process that enhances its nutritional value with bacteria vital for the digestive system, miso is considered the healthiest of soy-based foods. In one of the South Korean monasteries I visited, a large clay pot containing 10 year old miso stood in the center of the kitchen. White miso can be used to season salads or as a spread.

Healthy Winter Sandwich

材料

Yields 4

1 avocado, peeled

8 slices sour dough bread (recipe on page 50)

4 tsp. Indian Pesto (recipe on page 98)

1/4 cup broccoli sprouts

2 pickles in brine

4 arugula (rocket) leaves

2 Champignon mushrooms

1 carrot

4 Tbs. tahini paste

1/2 cup dill

Rinse and dry vegetables. Slice carrot into thin strips using a peeler. Cut mushrooms and pickles into thin slices. Cut avocado into strips. Chop dill and arugula. Assemble sandwiches: spread 4 slices of bread with tahini paste and the spread of your choice. Stack avocado, carrots, mushrooms and pickles, top with sprouts, dill and arugula. Close each sandwich with a slice of bread.

冬藏

163 | Winter

Tricolor Seaweed and Vegetable Winter Salad

材料

Serves 4

1 cup Hijiki

1 cup Wakame

1 cucumber

1 carrot

1 cup spinach

1/4 cup mint leaves

1 Tbs. white or black sesame seeds

Dressing

2 cloves garlic

2 Tbs. soy sauce

juice from 2 lemons

juice from 1 tangerine or orange

1/4 ginger root, grated

1/2 tsp. chili pepper

Soak seaweed in water for 15 minutes, rinse and drain. Rinse cucumber and carrot, discard ends and grate using a coarse grater, food processor fitted with grater or julienne peeler. Rinse and chop spinach and mint leaves. Place in a salad bowl. Add Wakame and remaining vegetables. In a food processor, process all dressing ingredients to a smooth, fully combined consistency. Pour over salad and sprinkle with sesame seeds.

Stir-fried Mushrooms, Bok choy and Endive on a Bed of Bulgur

材料

Serves 4

4 Shitake mushrooms

4 King Oyster mushrooms

4 Champignon mushrooms

4 bok choy leaves (substitute with Swiss chard or spinach)

4 scallions

4 endive leaves

4 sun-dried tomatoes

1 Tbs. soy sauce

1 Tbs. grated fresh ginger root

1 clove garlic

1 tsp. coarse Atlantic sea salt

1 tsp. ground black pepper

2 cups coarse bulgur

Soak bulgur in 2 cups water for 1 hour. Rinse and drain. Rinse all vegetables thoroughly. Stem mushrooms and cut into thin slices. Chop remaining vegetables. In a wok, stir-fry mushrooms in olive oil for 10 minutes. Add vegetables and spices. Stir-fry for 5 minutes. Serve over a bed of bulgur.

GOOD TO KNOW

King Oyster and Shitake mushrooms are staples in vegan cookery. Their meaty texture make them excellent fish substitutes. Due to their anti-cancer benefits, these mushrooms are widely used in Chinese medicine herb formulas.

GOOD TO KNOW

Vegan sushi can be prepared without rice. Using the traditional technique, place a leaf of Butterhead lettuce on Nori, add vegetables, and roll. This is a great recipe for those of us who have trouble digesting whole rice.

Gimbap – Korean Sushi

Yields 4 rolls

4 Nori sheet

2 cups whole short grained rice, cooked and chilled

1 tsp. sesame oil

1 tsp. soy sauce

1 tsp. sesame seeds

Umeboshi sauce, or Dijon mustard

1 scallion, julienned

1 cucumber, julienned

1 carrot, julienned

1/2 cup sunflower sprouts

1 avocado, cut into thin strips

50 gr. tofu, cut into strips, marinated in soy sauce, and steamed in the oven

fresh Shitake mushrooms, marinated in soy sauce, and steamed in the oven

1 red bell pepper, thinly sliced (optional)

Butterhead lettuce

pistachios and sunflower seeds

To serve

Wasabi

soy sauce

Rice preparation

Soak rice for 1 day. Drain and cover with water in a large pot. Bring to the boil, reduce heat and cook covered until the water is absorbed, approximately 40 minutes. Transfer rice to a bowl (preferably wooden). Add 1 tsp. each sesame oil and sesame seeds. Mix well.

Sushi Rolls

Place bamboo sushi mat on a clean surface. Place 1 Nori sheet on the mat, coarse side up. Using a wooden spoon, spread rice on the top half of the leaf, approximately 1/2 cm. thick. Arrange vegetables on the bottom quarter of the leaf. Top with lettuce to cover vegetables and approximately 1/3 third of the leaf. Sprinkle with pistachios and sunflower seeds. Dampen top edge of leaf. To roll: lift the sushi mat at the edge closest to you, roll half way. Next, separate mat from Nori, and roll once. Rotate mat so that exposed Nori is closest to you. Finally, press mat onto the entire length of the Nori. Remove roll from mat.

To serve

Using a sharp knife, cut roll in half. Cut each half in two, or into desired width. Serve with Wasabi and soy sauce.

Stuffed Mushrooms with
Macadamia Nut Cheese

材料

Serves 4

12 large Champignon or King Oyster mushrooms

Macadamia Nut Cheese

2 cups Macadamia nuts

6 sun-dried tomatoes

1/2 cup basil leaves

4 cloves garlic

1/4 cup olive oil

1 tsp. coarse Atlantic sea salt

pinch ground black pepper

GOOD TO KNOW

Professional chefs use paper towel to clean mushrooms without damaging their natural form and color. Originally, I prepared this recipe using goat cheese. Due to their meaty texture and 65% vegetable oil content, I often use ground macadamia nuts as a substitute for flour, dairy products and oil. Macadamia nuts are a recommended source of potassium and calcium.

Preheat oven to 180°C. Gently rinse mushrooms in cold water. Discard stems, leaving a cavity for stuffing. Process nuts and remaining ingredients in a food processor until creamy. Stuff mushrooms and arrange on a baking pan lined with parchment paper. Bake for 20 minutes.

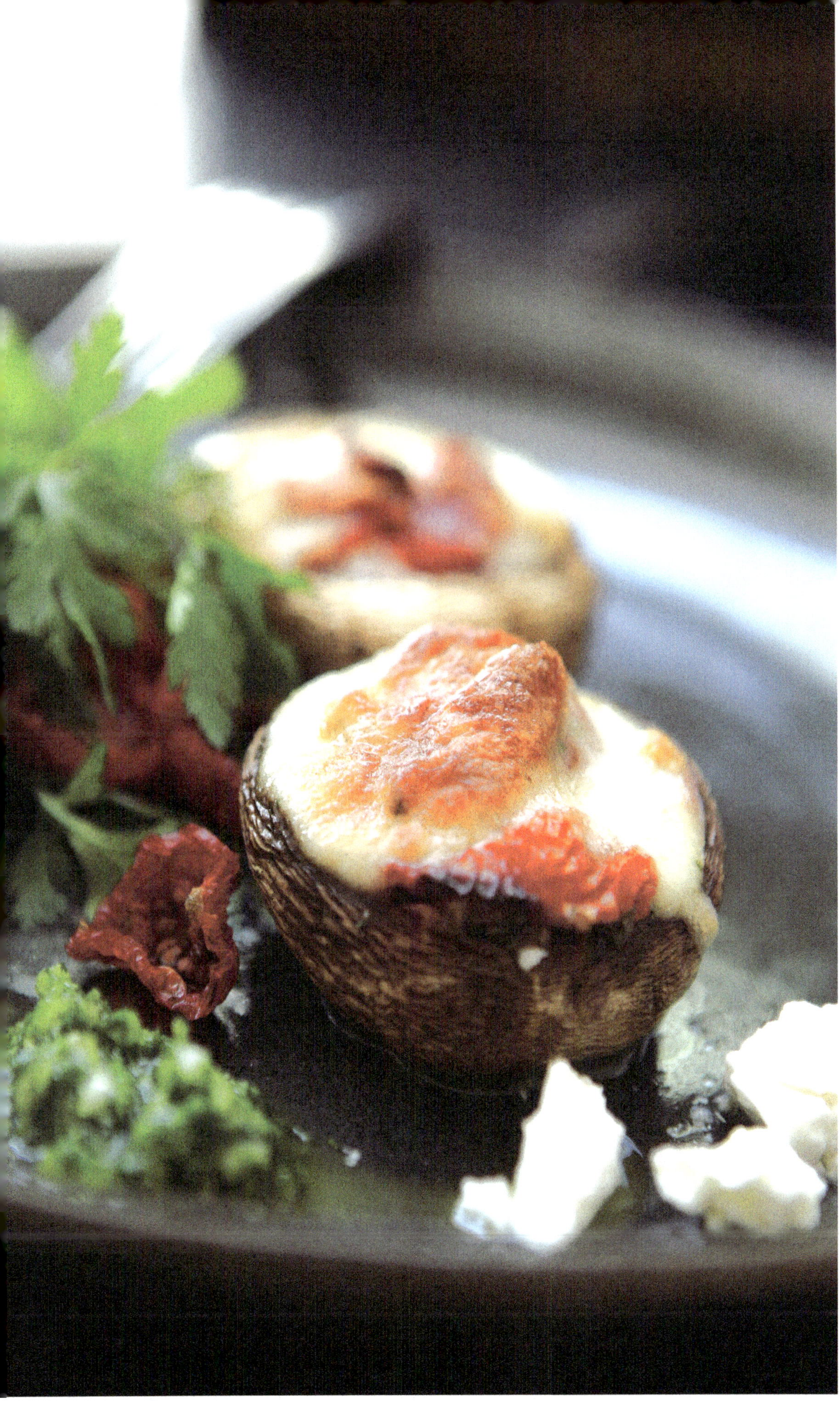

Mom's Homemade Chickpea Stew

Serves 4

500 gr. small dried chickpeas

1 large onion

6 cloves garlic

6 tomatoes

1 tsp. coarsely ground black pepper

1 tsp. turmeric (or 1 tsp. grated fresh turmeric root)

1 1/2 tsp. cumin

1 Tbs. coarse Atlantic sea salt

To serve

whole rice, whole couscous, cooked bulgur or barley

Soak chickpeas. Rinse and drain. To sprout, rinse and drain 3 times throughout the day.

Cook chickpeas in 3 liters water for 2 hours, or in a pressure cooker with 1 liter water for 1/2 hour. Drain. Reserve liquid.

Peel onion, chop and stir-fry with 1 Tbs. olive oil until golden. Rinse tomatoes and dice. Add to onions and sauté for 2 minutes. Add chickpeas, Spices and 4 cups reserved liquid. Bring to the boil, reduce heat and simmer, partially covered, for 1 1/2 hours. Serve on a bed of whole rice, whole couscous, bulgur or barley. For a perfect meal, serve with a spelt roll.

GOOD TO KNOW

One of my favorite childhood dishes, this stew is still a winner with family and friends. The combination of tomatoes, chickpeas and turmeric – a staple in Moroccan cooking – has a unique flavor, and is a rich source of essential proteins. According to philosopher Albertus Magnus, chickpeas have therapeutic attributes that enhance sperm count and quality, as well as increasing breast milk.

Spelt Rolls

In a mixing bowl, combine olive oil and maple syrup. Gradually add flour, oats, yeast and salt (if using an electric mixer, fit with a dough hook). Add water and knead for 10 minutes until dough is soft but not sticky. Cover bowl with a damp towel or plastic bag and keep in a warm place for 1 1/2 hours or 6 hours if using starter until dough is doubled in size. Transfer dough to a floured surface and divide into 25 balls. Knead each ball. Place balls on a baking sheet lined with parchment paper. Let rise for 30 minutes. Heat oven to 190°C. Sprinkle rolls with sesame seeds and salt. Bake for 20 minutes.

材料

Yields 25

1 kg. spelt flour

500 gr. sifted all-purpose flour

1 cup rolled oats

1 cup olive oil

1 Tbs. dry yeast
or 1 cup sourdough starter

1 tsp. maple syrup

4-5 cups
lukewarm water

1 Tbs. coarse
Atlantic sea salt

Garnish

black sesame seeds

coarse Atlantic
sea salt

174 | Five Seasons in the Kitchen

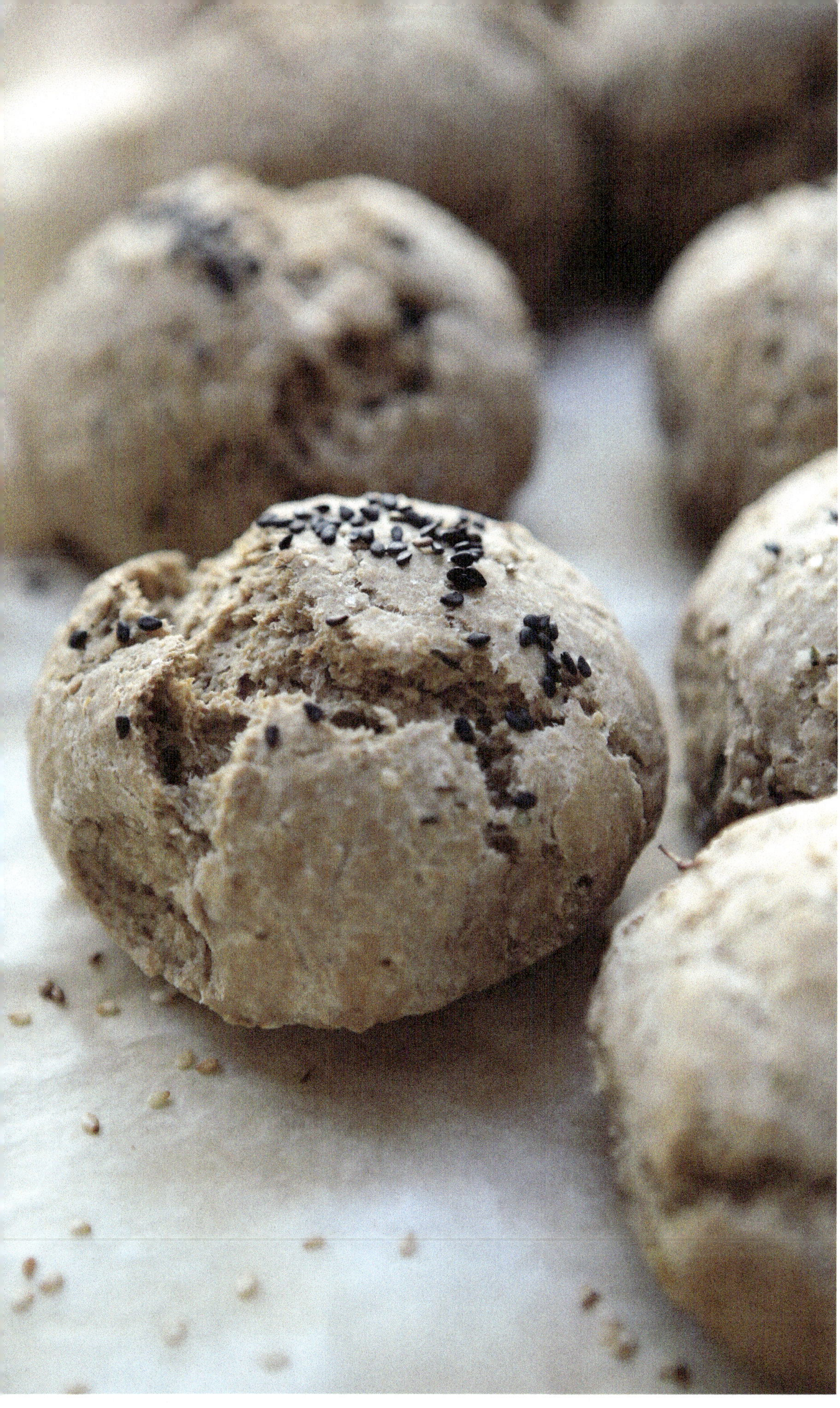

Root Vegetable and Tofu Stew

材料

Serves 2

2 leeks

50 gr. yellow lentils

2 cloves garlic

50 gr. tofu

1 kohlrabi

2 celery stalks

1 fennel

1 sweet potato

4 Portobello mushrooms

1 beet root

1 fresh chili peppers

1/2 Tbs. turmeric

2 tsp. coarsely ground black pepper

2 Tbs. soy sauce

100cc boiling water

Preheat oven to 200°C. Dice tofu and mix with soy sauce. Marinate for 1/2 hour. Rinse vegetables thoroughly; do not peel. Cut vegetables into 2 cm. cubes. Arrange tofu and vegetables in individual clay or iron cauldrons. Mix spices in boiling water and pour over vegetables. Bake for 40 minutes.

GOOD TO KNOW

Easy to prepare, stews are a wonderful way to keep warm on cold, winter days. I recommend using heavy cauldrons with tight fitting lids to ensure that ingredients cook in their own liquids. This recipe can be prepared outdoors using a cast iron pot placed directly on red hot coals.

Moroccan Style Jerusalem Artichokes

Serves 4

2 onions

3 cloves garlic

1 kg. Jerusalem artichokes

1 heaping Tbs. turmeric

1 tsp. ground caraway seeds

1 tsp. black pepper

1 heaping tsp. coarse Atlantic sea salt

1 Tbs. olive oil

Peel onion, rinse and chop. In a large pot, sauté in 1 Tbs. olive oil until lightly browned. Peel Jerusalem artichokes and cut into large cubes. Place artichokes in a large pot with garlic and spices. Bring to the boil, lower heat and cook for 45 minutes until artichokes are soft, but not mushy. Serve on a bed of whole rice.

GOOD TO KNOW

The Jerusalem artichoke is also known as sunroot. A staple in my mother's kitchen, this dish was my father's favorite. The recipe originated in Morocco where it is prepared with Cassava arrowroot and beef.

179 | Winter

GOOD TO KNOW

Korean cuisine features dozens of Kimchi varieties all of which contain chili. Kimchi is a traditional Korean dish, served with every meal. It is prepared in what Koreans call a "container" – a black clay kettle – commonly found in all Korean kitchens. Vegetable pickling, or fermentation, is a process in which "good" bacteria (lactobacillus) is released from the vegetables in an acidic environment. Due to this process, the vegetables' shelf life is significantly prolonged while maintaining their taste and nutrients (vitamins, minerals, enzymes and phytochemicals).

PICKLED VEGETABLES – KOREAN KIMCHI IN A PICKLING KETTLE

Cut cabbage into medium size pieces. Cut carrots and celery stalks on the angle into thin strips. Clean celery root and cut into medium size slices. Divide cauliflower into florets. Place all vegetables in a large bowl, add herbs, spices and water. Mix and transfer mixture to large, glass jars or a pickling kettle (sealed clay kettle, designed for pickling). Mark the preparation date on an adhesive label, and label jars or kettle. Place in a warm space (preferably in sunlight) for 3 days. Transfer to a shaded area for an additional 10 days.

材料

1 Chinese cabbage

1 cauliflower

4 celery roots

4 carrots

1 head celery

1 bunch fresh thyme

1 bunch oregano

i bunch tarragon

1 Tbs. "four seasons" pepper corns

8 Tbs. Atlantic sea coarse salt

10 cloves garlic

4 Tbs. Korean chili, hot paprika or chili pepper

5 bay leaves

4 liters water

GOOD TO KNOW

Tempeh is produced from fermented soy beans, making it one of the healthiest soy-based foods. To enhance its nutritional value, I recommend combining tempeh with a fresh vegetable or raw sprouts.

STIR-FRIED TEMPEH WITH JERUSALEM ARTICHOKES

In a wok, stir-fry tempeh with olive oil and curry until browned. Add Jerusalem artichokes and stir-fry until soft. Add pumpkin and stir-fry for 7 minutes, until slightly softened. Cut Swiss chard into medium sized strips, add to wok and stir-fry for 2 minutes. Remove from heat, add sprouts, soy sauce and chili oil. Splash with lemon juice, toss and serve.

Serves 4

1 package tempeh, diced

200 gr. pumpkin, peeled and diced

4 Swiss chard leaves, rinsed

4 Jerusalem artichokes, peeled and diced

1 package sunflower sprouts

1 tsp. curry powder

1 Tbs. olive oil

1 Tbs. soy sauce

1 tsp. chili oil

1/2 lemon

Bean, Lentil and Mushroom "Mesabaha"

Serves 4

1/2 cup white kidney beans (or any variety of white beans)

2 cups yellow lentils

1 tsp. turmeric

1 tsp. cumin

5 Shitake mushrooms

15 assorted mushrooms

1 onion

2 Tbs. soy sauce

1/2 tsp. black ground pepper

3 cloves garlic

1/2 chili pepper (optional)

1/4 cup dry red wine

juice from 2 limes or lemons

2 Tbs. coarse Atlantic sea salt

1/4 cup chopped peanuts

1/2 cup olive oil

Soak beans in water for 10 hours. Drain and transfer to colander to sprout for 24 hours, rinsing every 8 hours. Cook beans in a pressure cooker with 1 Tbs. salt and 3 cloves garlic for 1 1/2 hours, or in a regular pot for 3-4 hours on low heat until soft. Drain and grind to a coarse consistency in a food processor.

Rinse lentils and cook in 4 cups water seasoned with turmeric and cumin until water evaporates and lentils soften into a thick puree.

Chop onion and sauté in a wok with 2 Tbs. olive oil until lightly browned. Rinse mushrooms, chop and add to onion. Stir-fry until mushrooms are soft. Add soy sauce, black pepper and wine, and cook for 5-6 minutes.

Spread bean spread on serving dish, top with lentil spread and mushrooms. Sprinkle with chopped peanuts, drizzle with olive oil and lemon juice and serve.

This recipe was inspired by Chef Erez Komorovsky's hot bean spread served during a workshop held on a cold winter's day at his home in the Galilee. A variation on traditional "mesabaha" made with chickpeas, this combination of warm colors and deep flavors nurtures both body and soul. A particularly rich source of protein, this recipe is a welcome addition to vegan cookery.

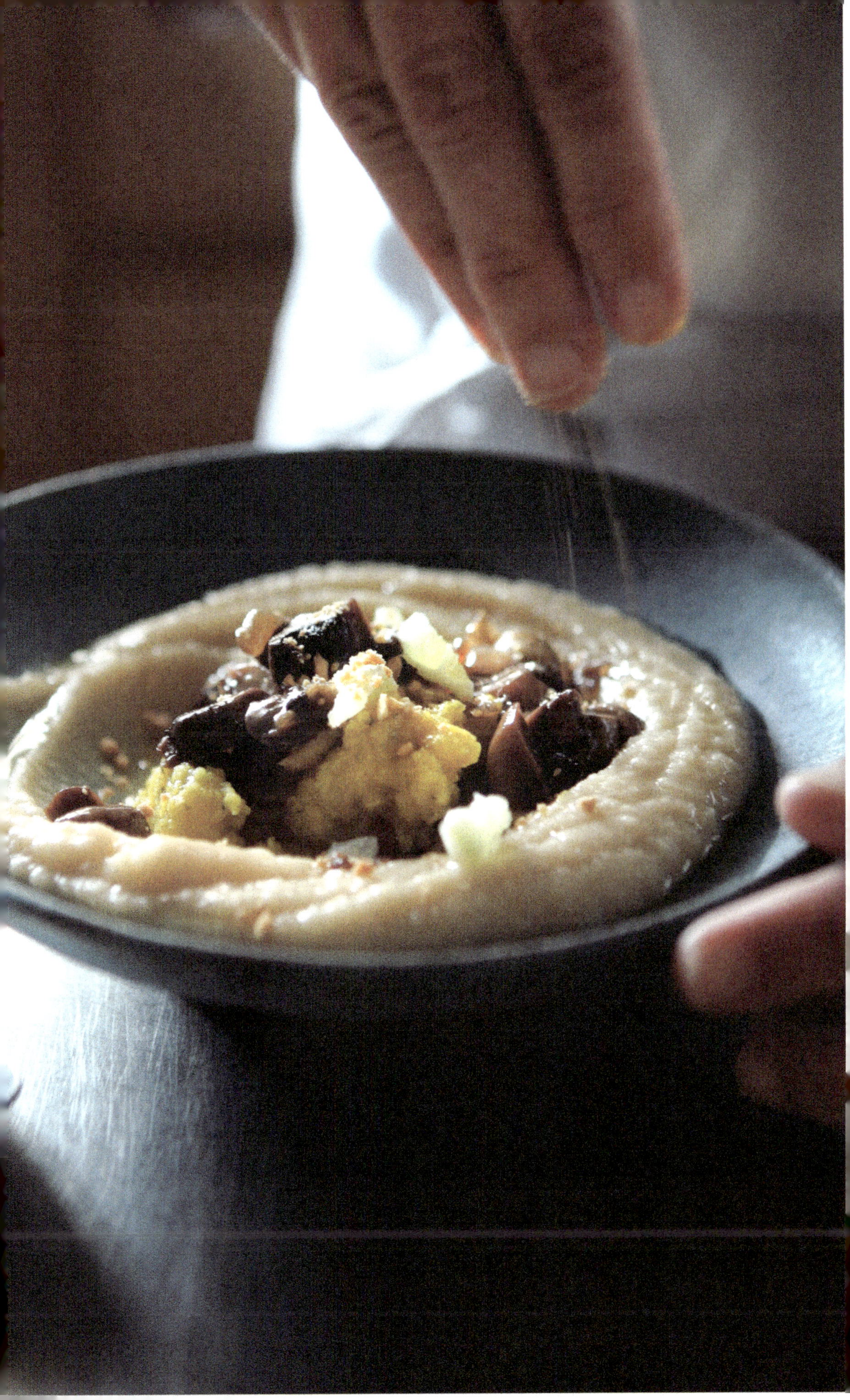

Rolled Oats Porridge

材料

Serves 4

16 Tbs. rolled oats

2 cups water

2 cups vanilla flavored rice milk, almond milk, or oat milk

4 Tbs. "cereal mix" (see recipe below)

4 tsp. sweetener (date honey, molasses or maple syrup)

Optional

1/2 cup diced seasonal fruit

Cereal Mix

Yields 1 liter

2 cups assorted dried fruit, diced into small cubes

2 cups ground almonds, walnuts and coconut

4 tsp. cinnamon

Cook oats, water, your choice of milk and sweetener for 15 minutes to desired consistency. Adding liquids and cooking for longer will yield a smooth, thinner porridge. Pour porridge into bowls, add cereal mix.

GOOD TO KNOW

Porridge is a staple food in the Far East. Highly nutritious, satisfying and economical, porridge is the conventional breakfast food in Zen monasteries.

187 | Winter

Spice Cake

24 cm. cake pan, or loaf pan

1 cup coconut oil

2 cups apple juice

1/2 cup date honey

2 cups spelt flour

1 Tbs. baking powder

1 cup raisins

1 cup pecans, finely ground

1 tsp. cinnamon

1 tsp. vanilla extract

4 bananas, mashed

zest from 1 lemon

1/2 cup ground cocoa beans

Preheat oven to 180°C. Mix all dry ingredients. in a mixing bowl. Gradually add liquid ingredients and beat until fully combined. Pour into baking pan. Bake for 1 1/2 hour.

Strawberry Sorbet

Place all ingredients in a blender. Blend until smooth and fully combined. Pour into silicon cube mold. Freeze. To serve: garnish with chocolate shavings and thin date slices.

材料

Yields 24 cubes

30 strawberries

1 Tbs. coconut oil

1 Tbs. organic maple syrup

Mindful Eating

Mindful eating is a conscious, delicate and calm approach to eating. It involves developing awareness of the nutrients available to us in the foods we eat, while acknowledging breathing, chewing and swallowing as integral parts of the eating experience. Mindful eating means respecting the needs of both body and soul, and devoting time to satisfy these needs. In harmony with what nature provides throughout the five seasons, eating mindfully engages the five senses: sight, smell, touch, sound and taste. Mindfulness cultivates our ability to make choices that are right for us, that help us feel healthier, more energetic, vital and happy. By being aware of what and how we eat, we are likely to eat less and better digest our food. As a result, our body weight is balanced, and we may even lose those extra pounds. But more importantly, we feel energized, focused and attuned to our inner wisdom.

Basic Rules for Mindful Eating

Chewing: to fully enjoy the foods we eat and digest them properly, we begin by responding to the various tastes and textures in our mouth as we chew. Chewing each bite approximately 40 times optimizes vitamin and mineral absorption and digestion.

Drinking: to avoid diluting digestive juices in the stomach, avoid drinking during and for 30 minutes following meals. A glass of quality wine, on the other hand, is a welcome accompaniment to any meal.

Fruit: eat a fruit approximately half an hour before, or one hour after, meals containing protein. The combination of fruit and protein induces fermentation in the digestive track.

Moderation: eat in moderation and only when you feel hungry. Try and consume one main meal a day.

Eating before bedtime: make every effort to stop eating four hours before going to bed for the night.

Variation: experiment with new and exciting recipes based on seasonal ingredients.

Bowel movements: bowel movements should be daily and regular, painless and without irregular odors.

Quality meal time: try and talk as little as possible during meals, do not answer the phone or engage in other activities. Devote quiet, calm time to eating; engage all of your senses and enjoy your food to the max!

The joy of preparation: any successful meal begins with the joy of creating it. While cooking, concentrate on what you are doing, be calm, relaxed and as cheerful as possible. Feel like artists in the kitchen, be excited, experiment with new ingredients and recipes, and most importantly, always season your meals with an abundance of love.

Juice cleanse: juice fasts or cleansings are the best way to cleanse your system. Twice a year, nurture your body with green shakes and clear fruit juices for three days. This is the best way to rest body, mind and soul.

For more information on juice fasts/cleanses go to www.avitality.co.il

Index

A

Açai berries
    Açai Sorbet 147

Açai Sorbet 147

Almonds
    Almond Milk 110
    Asparagus Wrapped in Seaweed with Tofu and Lemon Crumbs 62
    Baked Falafel 85
    Beet Pillows Stuffed with Almond-Sprout Spread 64
    Chilled Orange Almond Soup 110
    Comforting Homemade Chocolate 122
    Papaya Plus Smoothie 22
    Seasonal Fruit Ice Cream Cone Truffles 117

Almond Milk 110

Apples
    Papaya Plus Smoothie 22
    Sunny Winter Drink 157
    Won-Kwang-Sa Pie 114

Artichokes
    Green Bean and Snow Pea Salad with Purple Cabbage 32

Arugula (rocket)
    Fresh Tabbouleh Salad 29
    Healthy Winter Sandwich 162
    Spring Soba Noodle Salad 36

Asian Dressing
    Asian Papaya Salad 73
    Bite-size Beet and Zucchini Rolls 150

Asian Dressing 73

Asian Papaya Salad 73

Asparagus
    Asparagus Wrapped in Seaweed with Tofu and Lemon Crumbs 62
    Dough-free Asparagus Quiche 44
    Squash Flowers Stuffed with Mushrooms, Asparagus and Pine Nuts 78

Asparagus Wrapped in Seaweed with Tofu and Lemon Crumbs 62

Avocado
    Gimbap – Korean Sushi 169
    Green Bean and Snow Pea Salad with Purple Cabbage 32
    Healthy Winter Sandwich 162
    Vegetable Stuffed Persimmon Fruit Leather in Asian Sauce 27

B

Baked Cauliflower 67

Baked Falafel 85

Baked Vegetable Chips 69

Bananas
    Açai Sorbet 147
    Spice Cake 188

Basil
    Dough-free Asparagus Quiche 44
    Eggplant and Zucchini Rolls 148
    Endive Boats with Feta or Macadamia Nuts 60
    Indian Pesto 98
    Macadamia Nut Cheese 170
    Puccini Zucchini 102
    Rye and Spelt Flour Sicilian Pizza 42
    Spring Vegetable and Shallot Pie 46
    Stuffed Round Squash 106
    Sweet Potato Gnocchi with Grilled Pepper and Kalamata Olive Sauce 108

Basmati rice
    Colorful Paella with Fresh Shitake Mushrooms 136

    Whole Basmati Rice with Hijiki 38

Beans, kidney/white
    Bean, Lentil and Mushroom "Mesabaha" 184

Bean, Lentil and Mushroom "Mesabaha" 184

Beets
    Asian Papaya Salad 73

    Baked Vegetable Chips 69

    Beet Pillows Stuffed with Almond-Sprout Spread 64

    Bite-size Beet and Zucchini Rolls 150

    Endive Boats with Feta or Macadamia Nuts 60

    Root Vegetable and Tofu Stew 176

    Root Vegetables in Bamboo Steamer 103

    Vegetable Tofu Antipasti 128

Beet Pillows Stuffed with Almond-Sprout Spread 64

Bell peppers
    Colorful Paella with Fresh Shitake Mushrooms 136

    Gimbap - Korean Sushi 169

    Green Bean and Snow Pea Salad with Purple Cabbage 32

    Japanese Pickles 24

    Rye and Spelt Flour Sicilian Pizza 42

    Spring Tofu Sandwich 30

    Sweet Potato Gnocchi with Grilled Pepper and Kalamata Olive Sauce 108

    Three Variations on Tofu Kebabs 144

    Tri-color Cashew Cheese Rolls 97

    Vegetable Stuffed Persimmon Fruit Leather in Asian Sauce 27

    Vegetable Tofu Antipasti 128

    Yellow Lentil Soup with a Twist 158

Bite-size Beet and Zucchini Rolls 150

Black Rice Noodles
    Black Rice Noodles and Kohlrabi 76

Black Rice Noodles and Kohlrabi 76

Bok choy
    Stir-fried Mushrooms, Bok Choy and Endive on a Bed of Bulgur 166

Bright Orange Shake 94

Broad beans
    Broad Bean Spread 82

Broad Bean Spread 82

Broccoli
    Spring Soba Noodle Salad 36

    Spring Vegetable and Shallot Pie 46

Bulgur
    Fresh Tabbouleh Salad 29

    Stir-fried Mushrooms, Bok Choy and Endive on a Bed of Bulgur 166

C

Cabbage, Chinese
    Pickled Vegetables – Kimchi in a Pickling Kettle 181

Cabbage, green
    Traditional Couscous 134

Cabbage, purple
    Green Bean and Snow Pea Salad with Purple Cabbage 32

Carrot Soup with a Hint of Coconut 48

Carrots
    Asian Papaya Salad 73

    Bite-size Beet and Zucchini Rolls 150

Carrot Soup with a Hint of Coconut 48

Chilled Orange Almond Soup 110

Gimbap – Korean Sushi 169

Healthy Winter Sandwich 162

Japanese Pickles 24

Korean Miso Soup 160

Pickled Vegetables – Kimchi in a Pickling Kettle 181

Root Vegetables in Bamboo Steamer 103

Tricolor Seaweed and Vegetable Winter Salad 165

Vegetable Stuffed Persimmon Fruit Leather in Asian Sauce 27

Cashew nuts

Baked Falafel 85

Cauliflower and Pumpkin in Macadamia Cream 149

Nut Ice Cream Nuggets 88

Seasonal Fruit Ice Cream Cone Truffles 117

Spring Vegetable and Shallot Pie 46

Tri-color Cashew Cheese Rolls 97

Vegetable Stuffed Persimmon Fruit Leather in Asian Sauce 27

Cauliflower

Baked Cauliflower 67

Cauliflower and Pumpkin in Macadamia Cream 149

Hearty Root Soup 143

Pickled Vegetables – Kimchi in a Pickling Kettle 181

Spring Soba Noodle Salad 36

Traditional Couscous 134

Yellow Lentil Soup with a Twist 158

Cauliflower and Pumpkin in Macadamia Cream 149

Celery root

Carrot Soup with a Hint of Coconut 48

Hearty Root Soup 143

Korean Miso Soup 160

Pickled Vegetables – Kimchi in a Pickling Kettle 181

Traditional Couscous 134

Celery stalks

Carrot Soup with a Hint of Coconut 48

Chilled Orange Almond Soup 110

Colorful Paella with Fresh Shitake Mushrooms 136

Fresh Tabbouleh Salad 29

Green Bean and Snow Pea Salad with Purple Cabbage 32

Korean Miso Soup 160

Papaya Plus Smoothie 22

Pickled Vegetables – Kimchi in a Pickling Kettle 181

Root Vegetable and Tofu Stew 176

Traditional Couscous 134

Zucchini Salad with Champignon Mushrooms and Radish 104

Cereal Mix 186

Champignons

Healthy Winter Sandwich 162

Hearty Root Soup 143

Stir-fried Mushrooms, Bok Choy and Endive on a Bed of Bulgur 166

Stuffed Mushrooms with Macadamia Nut Cheese 170

Stuffed Round Squash 106

Three Way Toastini 70

Zucchini Salad with Champignon Mushrooms and Radish 104

Chestnuts
  Asian Papaya Salad 73

Chickpeas
  Mom's Homemade Chickpea Stew 172
  Shosh Kaviet's Hummus 80
  Traditional Couscous 134

Chili oil
  Asian Dressing 73
  Asian Papaya Salad 73
  Chilled Orange Almond Soup 110
  Stir-fried Tempeh with Jerusalem Artichokes 183
  Stuffed Round Squash 106
  Yellow Lentil Soup with a Twist 158

Chili pepper
  Baked Vegetable Chips 69
  Broad Bean Spread 82
  Chilled Orange Almond Soup 110
  Hearty Root Soup 143
  Indian Pesto 98
  Joy Crackers 100
  Pickled Vegetables – Kimchi in a Pickling Kettle 181
  Root Vegetable and Tofu Stew 176
  Spring Soba Noodle Salad 36
  Tricolor Seaweed and Vegetable Winter Salad 165
  Yellow Lentil Soup with a Twist 158

Chili pepper, Thai
  Vegetable Stuffed Persimmon Fruit Leather in Asian Sauce 27

Chili powder
  Colorful Paella with Fresh Shitake Mushrooms 136
  Tri-color Cashew Cheese Rolls 97

Chilled Orange Almond Soup 110

Chives
  Bite-size Beet and Zucchini Rolls 150
  Squash Flowers Stuffed with Mushrooms, Asparagus and Pine Nuts 78
  Sweet Potato Gnocchi with Grilled Pepper and Kalamata Olive Sauce 108
  Vegetable Stuffed Persimmon Fruit Leather in Asian Sauce 27

Chocolate 122

Cocoa powder
  Comforting Homemade Chocolate 122
  Milky Choco-Almond Shake 113
  Nut Ice Cream Nuggets 88
  Truffles 120

Coconut
  Truffles 120

Colorful Paella with Fresh Shitake Mushrooms 136

Comforting Homemade Chocolate 122

Coriander (cilantro)
  Asian Papaya Salad 73
  Colorful Paella with Fresh Shitake Mushrooms 136
  Endive Boats with Feta or Macadamia Nuts 60
  Hearty Root Soup 143
  Indian Pesto 98
  Spring Tofu Sandwich 30
  Traditional Couscous 134
  Vegetable Stuffed Persimmon Fruit Leather in Asian Sauce 27

Crackers 100

Creamy Lentil Soup 132

Cucumbers
  Bite-size Beet and Zucchini Rolls 150

Gimbap – Korean Sushi 169
Japanese Pickles 24
Three Way Toastini 70
Tricolor Seaweed and Vegetable Winter Salad 165
Whole Basmati Rice with Hijiki 38

D

Date honey
　Açai Sorbet 147
　Comforting Homemade Chocolate 122
　Pomacello Aperitif 146
　Rolled Oates Porridge 186
　Seasonal Fruit Ice Cream Cone Truffles 117
　Spice Cake 188
　Sunny Winter Drink 157

Dates
　Milky Choco-Almond Shake 113
　Nut Ice Cream Nuggets 88
　Papaya Plus Smoothie 22
　Won-Kwang-Sa Pie 114

Dill
　Green Bean and Snow Pea Salad with Purple Cabbage 32
　Healthy Winter Sandwich 162
　Japanese Pickles 24
　Three Way Toastini 70
　Whole Basmati Rice with Hijiki 38
Dough-free Asparagus Quiche 44

E

Eggplant
　Eggplant and Zucchini Rolls 148
　Roasted Eggplant in Tahini Paste 66
　Rye and Spelt Flour Sicilian Pizza 42
　Vegetable Tofu Antipasti 128
Eggplant and Zucchini Rolls 148

Endive
　Endive Boats with Feta or Macadamia Nuts 60
　Stir-fried Mushrooms, Bok Choy and Endive on a Bed of Bulgur 166
Endive Boats with Feta or Macadamia Nuts 60

F

Fennel
　Hearty Root Soup 143
　Root Vegetable and Tofu Stew 176
　Root Vegetables in Bamboo Steamer 103
　Yellow Lentil Soup with a Twist 158

Figs
　Bright Orange Shake 94

Flax seeds
　Baked Falafel 85
　Granola and Maple Syrup Cookies 52
　Joy Crackers 100
　Seasonal Fruit Ice Cream Cone Truffles 117
Fresh Tabbouleh Salad 29

G

Gimbap – Korean Sushi 169

Ginger root
　Beet Pillows Stuffed with Almond-Sprout Spread 64
　Black Rice Noodles and Kohlrabi 76
　Chilled Orange Almond Soup 110

Colorful Paella with Fresh Shitake Mushrooms 136

Creamy Lentil Soup 132

Hearty Root Soup 143

Japanese Pickles 24

King Oysters St. Jacques in Lemon Sauce 130

Pomacello Aperitif 146

Roasted Eggplant in Tahini Paste 66

Stir Fried Tofu with Seasonal Green Beans 139

Stir-fried Mushrooms, Bok Choy and Endive on a Bed of Bulgur 166

Sundried Tomatoes, Walnut and Ginger Spread 98

Sunny Winter Drink 157

Tricolor Seaweed and Vegetable Winter Salad 165

Goji berries

Comforting Homemade Chocolate 122

Fresh Tabbouleh Salad 29

Granola and Maple Syrup Cookies 52

Green beans

Green Bean and Snow Pea Salad with Purple Cabbage 32

Stir Fried Tofu with Seasonal Green Beans 139

Green Bean and Snow Pea Salad with Purple Cabbage 32

Green Salad with Mustard Miso Dressing 72

H

Healthy Winter Sandwich 162

Hearty Root Soup 143

Hemp oil

Pomegranate and Lime Drink 59

Herb salt 129

Hijiki

Colorful Paella with Fresh Shitake Mushrooms 136

Stir Fried Tofu with Seasonal Green Beans 139

Tricolor Seaweed and Vegetable Winter Salad 165

Whole Basmati Rice with Hijiki 38

Zucchini Salad with Champignon and Radish 104

Hummus Spread 80

I

Ice Cream 118

Ice Cream Cones 117

Indian Marinade 144

Indian Pesto 98

Indian Pesto 98

Bite-size Beet and Zucchini Rolls 150

Healthy Winter Sandwich 162

Spring Tofu Sandwich 30

Three Way Toastini 70

J

Japanese Pickles 24

Japanese radish

Green Bean and Snow Pea Salad with Purple Cabbage 32

Japanese Tofu Marinade 144

Jerusalem artichoke

Moroccan Style Jerusalem Artichokes 178

Stir-fried Tempeh with Jerusalem Artichokes 183

Vegetable Tofu Antipasti 128

Joy Crackers 100

Juju's Sourdough Bread 50

K

Kalamata olives
 Dough-free Asparagus Quiche 44
 Endive Boats with Feta or Macadamia Nuts 60
 Puccini Zucchini 102
 Sweet Potato Gnocchi with Grilled Pepper and Kalamata Olive Sauce 108

King Oyster mushrooms
 Colorful Paella with Fresh Shitake Mushrooms 136
 King Oysters St. Jacques in Lemon Sauce 130
 Spring Vegetable and Shallot Pie 46
 Stir Fried Tofu with Seasonal Green Beans 139
 Stir-fried Mushrooms, Bok Choy and Endive on a Bed of Bulgur 166
 Stuffed Mushrooms with Macadamia Nut Cheese 170

King Oysters St. Jacques in Lemon Sauce 130

Kobo
 Pomegranate and Lime Drink 59

Kohlrabi
 Black Rice Noodles and Kohlrabi 76
 Japanese Pickles 24
 Root Vegetable and Tofu Stew 176
 Root Vegetables in Bamboo Steamer 103
 Vegetable Tofu Antipasti 128

Kombu seaweed
 Korean Miso Soup 160

Korean Miso Soup 160

L

Lady Fingers 86

Leeks
 Carrot Soup with a Hint of Coconut 48
 Colorful Paella with Fresh Shitake Mushrooms 136
 Dough-free Asparagus Quiche 44
 Root Vegetable and Tofu Stew 176
 Traditional Couscous 134
 Yellow Lentil Soup with a Twist 158

Lentils
 Baked Falafel 85
 Bean, Lentil and Mushroom "Mesabaha" 184
 Creamy Lentil Soup 132
 Root Vegetable and Tofu Stew 176
 Sprouted Lentil and Walnut Spread 98
 Yellow Lentil Soup with a Twist 158

Lettuce
 Gimbap – Korean Sushi 169
 Green Salad with Mustard Miso Dressing 72
 Papaya Plus Smoothie 22

Lime
 Açai Sorbet 147
 Asian Dressing 73
 Asian Papaya Salad 73
 Bean, Lentil and Mushroom "Mesabaha" 184
 Bright Orange Shake 94
 Fresh Tabbouleh Salad 29
 Pomegranate and Lime Drink 59
 Sunny Winter Drink 157

M

Macadamia Nut Cheese
 Dough-free Asparagus Quiche 44
 Eggplant and Zucchini Rolls 148

Rye and Spelt Flour Sicilian Pizza 42

Spring Vegetable and Shallot Pie 46

Squash Flowers Stuffed with Mushrooms, Asparagus and Pine Nuts 78

Stuffed Mushrooms with Macadamia Nut Cheese 170

Macadamia Nut Cheese 170

Macadamia nuts

Cauliflower and Pumpkin in Macadamia Cream 149

Endive Boats with Feta or Macadamia Nuts 60

Macadamia Nut Cheese 170

Stuffed Round Squash 106

Mango

Açai Sorbet 147

Bright Orange Shake 94

Maple syrup

Spelt Rolls 174

Comforting Homemade Chocolate 122

Granola and Maple Syrup Cookies 52

Milky Choco-Almond Shake 113

Nut Ice Cream Nuggets 88

Persimmon Sorbet 52

Pomacello Aperitif 146

Rolled Oates Porridge 186

Rye and Spelt Flour Sicilian Pizza 42

Strawberry Sorbet 189

Truffles 120

Won-Kwang-Sa Pie 114

Mediterranean Tofu Marinade 144

Milky Choco-Almond Shake 113

Mint sprigs/leaves

Bright Orange Shake 94

Fresh Tabbouleh Salad 29

Indian Pesto 98

Papaya Plus Smoothie 22

Pomegranate and Lime Drink 59

Seasonal Fruit Ice Cream Cone Truffles 117

Tricolor Seaweed and Vegetable Winter Salad 165

Mirin

Zucchini Salad with Champignon Mushrooms and Radish 104

Miso

Cauliflower and Pumpkin in Macadamia Cream 149

Green Salad with Mustard Miso Dressing 72

Korean Miso Soup 160

Mom's Homemade Chickpea Stew 172

Moroccan Style Jerusalem Artichokes 178

Mushrooms, assorted

Bean, Lentil and Mushroom "Mesabaha" 184

Squash Flowers Stuffed with Mushrooms, Asparagus and Pine Nuts 78

Vegetable Stuffed Persimmon Fruit Leather in Asian Sauce 27

Mustard Miso Dressing 72

N

Nigella seed oil

Asian Dressing 73

Asian Papaya Salad 73

Nori sheets

Asparagus Wrapped in Seaweed with Tofu and Lemon Crumbs 62

Gimbap – Korean Sushi 169

Nut Ice Cream Nuggets 88

O

Oats, rolled
   Spelt Rolls 174
   Rolled Oates Porridge 186

Oranges
   Green Bean and Snow Pea Salad with Purple Cabbage 32
   Persimmon Sorbet 52
   Sunny Winter Drink 157
   Tricolor Seaweed and Vegetable Winter Salad 165

P

Papaya
   Papaya Plus Smoothie 22

Papaya Plus Smoothie 22

Papaya, green
   Asian Papaya Salad 73

Parsley root
   Carrot Soup with a Hint of Coconut 48
   Hearty Root Soup 143
   Korean Miso Soup 160
   Traditional Couscous 134

Pears
   Pomegranate and Lime Drink 59
   Seasonal Fruit Ice Cream Cone Truffles 117

Persimmons
   Persimmon Sorbet 52
   Vegetable Stuffed Persimmon Fruit Leather in Asian Sauce 27

Persimmon Sorbet 52

Pickled Vegetables – Kimchi in a Pickling Kettle 181

Pomacello Aperitif 146

Pomegranate syrup
   Pomegranate and Lime Drink 59

Pomegranates
   Pomegranate and Lime Drink 59
   Pomacello Aperitif 146

Pomegranate and Lime Drink 59

Portobello mushrooms
   Root Vegetable and Tofu Stew 176
   Stir Fried Tofu with Seasonal Green Beans 139

Puccini Zucchini 102

Pumpkin
   Cauliflower and Pumpkin in Macadamia Cream 149
   Root Vegetables in Bamboo Steamer 103
   Rye and Spelt Flour Sicilian Pizza 42
   Stir-fried Tempeh with Jerusalem Artichokes 183
   Traditional Couscous 134

Q

Quinoa
   Fresh Tabbouleh Salad 29

R

Radishes
   Japanese Pickles 24
   Spring Tofu Sandwich 30
   Zucchini Salad with Champignon Mushrooms and Radish 104

Rice malt
   Comforting Homemade Chocolate 122
   Truffles 120

Roasted Eggplant in Tahini Paste 66
Rolled Oates Porridge 186
Root Vegetable and Tofu Stew 176
Root Vegetables in Bamboo Steamer 103
Rye and Spelt Flour Sicilian Pizza 42

S

Sambal, Asian okra
    Lady Fingers 86

Scallions
    Bite-size Beet and Zucchini Rolls 150
    Black Rice Noodles and Kohlrabi 76
    Gimbap – Korean Sushi 169
    Green Bean and Snow Pea Salad with Purple Cabbage 32
    Spring Pyramid with Artichoke 34
    Spring Soba Noodle Salad 36
    Stir-fried Mushrooms, Bok Choy and Endive on a Bed of Bulgur 166

Seasonal Fruit Ice Cream Cone Truffles 117

Shallots
    Cauliflower and Pumpkin in Macadamia Cream 149
    Spring Vegetable and Shallot Pie 46
    Three Variations on Tofu Kebabs 144

Shitake mushrooms
    Bean, Lentil and Mushroom "Mesabaha" 184
    Colorful Paella with Fresh Shitake Mushrooms 136
    Gimbap - Korean Sushi 169
    Korean Miso Soup 160
    Stir Fried Tofu with Seasonal Green Beans 139
    Stir-fried Mushrooms, Bok Choy and Endive on a Bed of Bulgur 166

Shosh Kaviet's Hummus 80

Snow peas
    Green Bean and Snow Pea Salad with Purple Cabbage 32

Sour dough bread
    Healthy Winter Sandwich 162
    Spring Tofu Sandwich 30

Sourdough Bread 50
Spice Cake 188

Spelt flour
    Spelt Rolls 174
    Granola and Maple Syrup Cookies 52
    Juju's Sourdough Bread 50
    Rye and Spelt Flour Sicilian Pizza 42
    Seasonal Fruit Ice Cream Cone Truffles 117
    Spring Vegetable and Shallot Pie 46
    Sweet Potato Gnocchi with Grilled Pepper and Kalamata Olive Sauce 108

Spelt Rolls 174

Spinach
    Green Bean and Snow Pea Salad with Purple Cabbage 32
    Spring Vegetable and Shallot Pie 46
    Stir-fried Mushrooms, Bok Choy and Endive on a Bed of Bulgur 166
    Tricolor Seaweed and Vegetable Winter Salad 165

Spring Pyramid with Artichoke 34
Spring Soba Noodle Salad 36
Spring Tofu Sandwich 30
Spring Vegetable and Shallot Pie 46
Sprouted Lentil and Walnut Spread
    Three Way Toastini 70
Sprouted Lentil and Walnut Spread 98

Sprouts, Broccoli

    Beet Pillows Stuffed with Almond-Sprout Spread 64

    Carrot Soup with a Hint of Coconut 48

    Healthy Winter Sandwich 162

Sprouts, Mung bean

    Bite-size Beet and Zucchini Rolls 150

    Korean Miso Soup 160

    Vegetable Stuffed Persimmon Fruit Leather in Asian Sauce 27

    Yellow Lentil Soup with a Twist 158

Sprouts, Radish

    Asparagus Wrapped in Seaweed with Tofu and Lemon Crumbs 62

Sprouts, Sunflower

    Bite-size Beet and Zucchini Rolls 150

    Gimbap – Korean Sushi 169

    Spring Tofu Sandwich 30

    Stir-fried Tempeh with Jerusalem Artichokes 183

    Vegetable Stuffed Persimmon Fruit Leather in Asian Sauce 27

Squash

    Root Vegetables in Bamboo Steamer 103

    Stuffed Round Squash 106

Squash flowers

    Squash Flowers Stuffed with Mushrooms, Asparagus and Pine Nuts 78

Squash Flowers Stuffed with Mushrooms, Asparagus and Pine Nuts 78

Stir-fried Tofu with Seasonal Green Beans 139

Stir-fried Mushrooms, Bok Choy and Endive on a Bed of Bulgur 166

Stir-fried Tempeh with Jerusalem Artichokes 183

Strawberries

    Papaya Plus Smoothie 22

    Strawberry Sorbet 189

Strawberry Sorbet 189

Stuffed Mushrooms with Macadamia Nut Cheese 170

Stuffed Round Squash 106

Sundried Tomatoes, Walnut and Ginger Spread 98

Sunny Winter Drink 157

Sweet potato

    Baked Vegetable Chips 69

    Root Vegetable and Tofu Stew 176

    Root Vegetables in Bamboo Steamer 103

    Sweet Potato Gnocchi with Grilled Pepper and Kalamata Olive Sauce 108

    Vegetable Tofu Antipasti 128

Sweet Potato Gnocchi with Grilled Pepper and Kalamata Olive Sauce 108

Swiss chard

    Green Bean and Snow Pea Salad with Purple Cabbage 32

    Stir-fried Mushrooms, Bok Choy and Endive on a Bed of Bulgur 166

    Stir-fried Tempeh with Jerusalem Artichokes 183

T

Tahini paste

    Asparagus Wrapped in Seaweed with Tofu and Lemon Crumbs 62

    Baked Falafel 85

    Beet Pillows Stuffed with Almond-Sprout Spread 64

    Healthy Winter Sandwich 162

    Roasted Eggplant in Tahini Paste 66

    Root Vegetables in Bamboo Steamer 103

Shosh Kaviet's Hummus 80

Tangerine

Tricolor Seaweed and Vegetable Winter Salad 165

Tempeh

Stir-fried Tempeh with Jerusalem Artichokes 183

Three Variations on Tofu Kebabs 144

Three Way Toastini 70

Tofu

Asparagus Wrapped in Seaweed with Tofu and Lemon Crumbs 62

Colorful Paella with Fresh Shitake Mushrooms 136

Gimbap - Korean Sushi 169

Green Bean and Snow Pea Salad with Purple Cabbage 32

Korean Miso Soup 160

Root Vegetable and Tofu Stew 176

Spring Tofu Sandwich 30

Stir Fried Tofu with Seasonal Green Beans 139

Three Variations on Tofu Kebabs 144

Three Way Toastini 70

Vegetable Tofu Antipasti 128

Tomatoes

Baked Falafel 85

Colorful Paella with Fresh Shitake Mushrooms 136

Creamy Lentil Soup 132

Green Bean and Snow Pea Salad with Purple Cabbage 32

Lady Fingers 86

Mom's Homemade Chickpea Stew 172

Puccini Zucchini 102

Rye and Spelt Flour Sicilian Pizza 42

Squash Flowers Stuffed with Mushrooms, Asparagus and Pine Nuts 78

Tomatoes, sun-dried

Dough-free Asparagus Quiche 44

Endive Boats with Feta or Macadamia Nuts 60

Green Bean and Snow Pea Salad with Purple Cabbage 32

Joy Crackers 100

Macadamia Nut Cheese 170

Puccini Zucchini 102

Rye and Spelt Flour Sicilian Pizza 42

Sprouted Lentil and Walnut Spread 98

Stir-fried Mushrooms, Bok Choy and Endive on a Bed of Bulgur 166

Sundried Tomatoes, Walnut and Ginger Spread 98

Three Way Toastini 70

Tri-color Cashew Cheese Rolls 97

Traditional Couscous 134

Tri-color Cashew Cheese Rolls 97

Tricolor Seaweed and Vegetable Winter Salad 165

Truffles 120

Turkish spinach

Green Salad with Mustard Miso Dressing 72

Turnip

Traditional Couscous 134

Vegetable Tofu Antipasti 128

U

Umeboshi sauce

Beet Pillows Stuffed with Almond-Sprout Spread 64

Gimbap – Korean Sushi 169

Japanese Pickles 24

V

Vanilla extract
- Nut Ice Cream Nuggets 88
- Seasonal Fruit Ice Cream Cone Truffles 117
- Spice Cake 188
- Truffles 120

Vegetable Stuffed Persimmon Fruit Leather in Asian Sauce 27

Vegetable Tofu Antipasti 128

W

Wakame seaweed
- Korean Miso Soup 160
- Tricolor Seaweed and Vegetable Winter Salad 165

Whole Basmati Rice with Hijiki 38

Won-Kwang-Sa Pie 114

Yellow Lentil Soup with a Twist 158

Z

Zucchini
- Baked Vegetable Chips 69
- Bite-size Beet and Zucchini Rolls 150
- Eggplant and Zucchini Rolls 148
- Puccini Zucchini 102
- Rye and Spelt Flour Sicilian Pizza 42
- Three Variations on Tofu Kebabs 144
- Traditional Couscous 134
- Vegetable Stuffed Persimmon Fruit Leather in Asian Sauce 27
- Zucchini Salad with Champignon Mushrooms and Radish 104

Zucchini Salad with Champignon Mushrooms and Radish 104

Notes

禅

Notes

禅

Notes

禅

210 | Five Seasons in the Kitchen

Thank You

多谢

To my beloved Family: My dear mother Simcha and my late father Gabi Sebbag, of Blessed Memory. To Doron & Adi Sebbag and the entire ORS family, my sister Dorit Gellerman-Sebbag. To my amazing sons Yossi, Mikey, Gabriel "Babi", Joy & Yonatan. To Yuli and Tati Hava. To my extended family aunts, uncles, cousins, nieces and nephews. To the entire Sebbag-Toledano-Zafrani families for my Moroccan roots and upbringing.

A big thank you to the amazing production crew, for your assistance throughout this journey, your trust and support. Thank you to the talented photographer Michal Lenart. Thanks to my wonderful friends Efrat Marciano (Mor) and Orit Rahmani, Tamar Mor-Sela, Ingrid Kutner, Elza Puin and Diane Ayoun, Cathrine Gerson for the index and Elizabeth Zauderer for the English translation.

To the Kwan um school of Zen: A special thanks to my dearest Zen teacher Yuval Gil and his remarkable mother Rowena, thanks to you I found my way.

Zen master Soeng Hyang, Zen Master Wu Bong in Memory, Zen Master Dae Jin in Memory, Zen Master Bon Shim, Jo Potter JDPSN, Zen Master Ji Kwang, Zen Master Dae Bong, To all the Sangha for allowing me to grant presents from my kitchen, cooking retreats and special occasions.

To my partner, Zohar Zemach Wilson on our joined voyage. Ruthi Roi-Weinstein (Taatzomot), Anat Tzahor (Yoga Dharma), Efrat Abramson, Ida Tzitzula, Revital and Shahar Lev Ari, Renana Lee-Horesh, Tammy Hahn, Lior Hikri, Dafna Botzer, Tamar Tzoberi, Shimi, Nomind, the Moa Oasis Family, Ayala Rish-Lakish, Zipi Pukka-Israel, Ori BioGreen, Niv Jammoka, Yossi Kefir - King Solomon Wisdom.

A special thank you to my dearest friends: Yahli Admati, Ruth Leshem, Roni Oren, Daphna and Danny Abraham, Amalia Lazrov, Jackie Waik, Bella Blum (RIP), Simcha Ziv (RIP), Gili Ben Ami (RIP), and Shosh Cviat (RIP). Shira Levy, Eran Barkan, Esty and Oren "the Important Man", Nava Siman Tov.

Thanks to all those who contributed products, kitchenware, clothing and accessories: Tema Design, Tamarindi, Hibino, Kneh Kash, Ayelet Guy Curtain Studio, Nook Atmosphere, Hercules Parquet, Daphna Butcher Pottery, Billy Chinese Pottery.

Special thanks to my talented friend Eddie Goldfine, for designing this book and for his friendship. And to all my friends, students and teachers along the way.